LIVING

A HAPPIER

LIFE

AT EVERY AGE!

Rev. Dr. John H. Krahn

krahns@msn.com

Living A Happier Life – At Every Age!

Copyright 2018 by John H. Krahn Publishing Co.

All rights reserved.

All biblical quotations are taken from the New Revised Standard Version.

Additional books are available from Amazon.com or email krahns@msn.com and ask for information on a discounted price.

Library of Congress Cataloging-in-Publication Data is available.

ISBN-13: 978-1973994121

ISBN-10: 1973994127

OTHER TITLES BY
JOHN H. KRAHN

Love – It's the Greatest!

Special Stories Along Life's Journey

Brief Prayers for Busy Lives

From Surviving to Thriving -
A Practical Guide to Revitalize Your Church

Seasonings for Sermons III

Washed Any Feet Lately?

Reaching the Inactive Member

Ministry Ideabank

Ministry Ideabank II

Ministry Ideabank III

DEDICATION

This book is dedicated to my Lord Jesus Christ who has loved me unconditionally. It is also dedicated to those people throughout my long life who have loved me and made my life happier. These include my wife, children, grandchildren, sons-in-law, parents, sister, brother-in-law, mother and father-in-law, grandparents, aunts, uncles, cousins, nephews, nieces, mentors and friends. For each and every one of them, I am eternally grateful.

CONTENTS

INTRODUCTION

Who does not desire a little more happiness in their life? It is impossible for anyone to be too happy. There is so much in life that erodes our happiness that a happiness tune up is always in order. This is why I wrote *Living a Happier Life – At Every Age!* It considers many different aspects of your life where a better understanding and a different attitude will help you live a happier life. Do you find yourself worrying too much? Are life's challenges and hurts piling up on you? Do you sometimes feel worthless? Have you ever wondered why there is so much suffering in the world? These are just some of the questions this book seeks to answer.

Living a Happier Life also looks at how you might make a difference with your life. It encourages a "can do" spirit as you tackle life's challenges. Prayer and forgiveness are presented as vehicles to a happier life. As you grow older, you are shown how to do it with grace. Then, as you step from this life into eternity, you will learn how to do this with both peaceful acceptance and joy. Pure happiness awaits you in the presence of God. You are heaven bound through believing in the Lord Jesus Christ. The happiest time in your life is still awaiting you.

Happiness doesn't come so much from that which is outside of you, but it emanates from what is inside of you. The wealthiest people in the world are those who have discovered how to be happy. It is not a matter of how much we have but how much we enjoy what we have. One's attitude must be one of gratitude in order to be happy.

This book has come out of a life blessed with longevity and the pleasure of working with thousands of people as a clergy. It is not a philosophical treatise but a practical guide on how to pursue a happier life. Since happiness is something to share as well, please tell others about this book. It can also be effectively used in an Adult Christian Education discussion group. I hope you will be blessed by reading it and that it puts a smile on your face.

I wish to especially thank Doris Krahn, JoAnn Breitbach, Evelyn Andersen Meyers, Jane Kerr, Emme Gannon, Dr. Astrid Sipos, and Dr. Elsie Szecsy for doing a careful job of proofreading and making thoughtful suggestions which have improved this book.

ONE

CHOOSE A HAPPIER LIFE

Who wouldn't want to have some of the wealth of The Donald? In the past, I watched Donald Trump on his former television show, "The Apprentice," and the man didn't seem all that happy. I think that another Donald I know is much happier. He is a young man who works for our local supermarket collecting the shopping carts left in the parking lot. He has been doing this part-time job for years. He is always smiling and has a big cheery, happy greeting for everyone.

Recently I engaged our local supermarket Donald in conversation asking him if he worked every day. "No way," he answered, "I need time to play with my kids." This surprised me, for he seemed to be a bit slow of mind, so I asked him if he indeed had children. "I play with the kids in the neighborhood; these are my kids," he responded. "Do you live with your parents?" I continued. "No, I have my own room that I rent. I don't need much. Actually I spend very little money, for I don't have a T.V. and all those gadgets everyone else has. I can make my money go very far."

If The Donald is one of the men who owns the most in worldly possessions, our supermarket Donald is among those folks who own the very least. But from all outward appearances, supermarket Donald has chosen to not let his limited income define his happiness. He is clearly a person who chooses to be happy every day.

I am old enough to have known people who lived through the Great Depression. Many times I've heard these people say, "We were really poor but did not realize how poor we were at the time. In spite of it, I had a happy childhood." Having more stuff does not equate with more happiness. More than half of the folks who won big playing the lottery have indicated that they were less happy after winning. The reason that I never buy a lottery ticket is because I do <u>not</u> want to win. If the odds are greater that winning will make me unhappy, then why would I want to take that chance?

Granted, having food and shelter and life's basics are important for all of us and going to bed hungry is never a happy situation. But much more beyond this leads to the question of how much is really enough? For many, enough is defined as having a little bit more than they currently have. If having more is the source of happiness, then when they get more they will still not be happy because they will still want a little more than that. Continually striving for more does not seem like a very happy life style to me.

The story is told of a grandmother who is walking her grandson along the beach, hat on head protecting him from the sun. A big unexpected wave suddenly washes over the boy and pulls him screaming out to sea. The boy will surely die. Unable to swim herself, the grandmother   falls on her knees in fervent prayer begging God to save him.

Immediately, another large wave comes into shore and deposits the boy safely at her feet. Wiping the sand off the boy and seeing that he is all right, she observes that his hat is gone. She again turns her face heavenward and snaps, "And so what became of my grandson's hat?" Being abundantly blessed by the safe return of her grandson was not enough for her; the ungrateful woman complains about a silly, lost hat. Is there a similar story from our lives?

We really have little control over much of what happens in our lives. We did not choose our parents. We did not choose our country of birth. We had no say over our intelligence quotient. We haven't had many of the diseases that are common in most of the world. Much of our good fortune has been the result of being at the right place at the right time. Much in our lives is out of our control. What we can control is how we respond to what happens in our lives. Our attitude has a lot to do with how we let life affect us. Life is not so much what life brings our way, but the attitude we bring to our life.

An Attitude of Gratitude

All of us have an attitude. Our attitude is our mental position that triggers how we respond to what happens in our lives. When we say that people have an "attitude," we usually mean that they have a chip on their shoulder. But attitude is not negative in and of itself. It is neutral. We can have a negative attitude, but we can just as well have a healthy, positive attitude when approaching life. Do we approach life with an attitude which seeks to find the good in every situation? Are we thankful for what we have rather than unhappy about what we don't have?

One of the greatest disabilities in life is having a negative attitude. An attitude of gratitude is a happy attitude. A positive attitude produces positive thoughts and outcomes. We can choose to be happy or choose to be unhappy. It is not a matter of how much we have, it's how much we appreciate what we have. Henry David Thoreau, the American naturalist and philosopher, used to lie in bed each morning telling himself all the good news he could remember. When he got up, he was ready to meet a world filled with so many good things, good people, and good opportunities.

I have been privileged during my lifetime to know one of the wealthiest people in the world. He wasn't a Rockefeller, a Bezos, or a Gates. He was a simple custodian for much of his life in a public elementary school. He happened to be my father-in-law and my children's Opa. The man enjoyed his simple life to the fullest. Ah, the wonderful taste of a jelly donut from Tilda's, the local bakery. Opa relished seeing my young children enjoy one of Tilda's overstuffed jelly donuts, so that when they took their first bite, the jelly exploded and spilled down their chins. Opa also loved to spot and lay claim to a discarded treasure along the road. When facing a problem, the man would always proclaim in his German accent, "Everytang gonna be all right." The man was thankful in all things. This man had an attitude . . . an attitude of gratitude. He was the wealthiest person I have ever known.

A grateful heart measures its wealth by what it has rather than by what it lacks. If children can be excited by a few trinkets in their Christmas stockings, should we not be grateful that God gives us two healthy legs to put in our stockings every day? There is always someone who has more than we do. We can always find someone whose life seems better than ours. But this is seeing our lives out of focus. We must see the cups of our lives as not being just half full but as overflowing.

Choose Happiness

One day I asked Linda, a friend of mine, who was always happy, what her secret was. She simply replied, "I choose to be happy." I discovered that she had been a single mother for years. Earlier in her life, her two children were playing in the street. A neighborhood teenager hit both children and killed her son. The stress of this tragic loss caused the dissolution of her marriage. When I met her years later, she was struggling with stage three cancer. She had lost all her hair and permanently wore a wig. A tragic loss of a child, a divorce, and cancer, and this woman was one of the most upbeat people I knew. In spite of it all, she chose to live a happy life.

If you wish a better life, choose to see your life as better. Happiness is a blessing that comes to those who daily beckon her. Wake up each morning and intend today to be a better day than yesterday. Begin the day by saying, "I am going to be happy in spite of. . . ." And remember that a smile is the least expensive way to instantly improve your looks. An old saying comes readily to mind, "Yesterday is history, tomorrow is a mystery, today is a gift from God, that is why it is called the present." There is nothing we can do to change yesterday's mistakes and lost opportunities. We simply must offer them up to a merciful God. Who among us can be so arrogant to be certain that we will see tomorrow? All we have is today, the present, to live to its fullest no matter what challenges or problems we face in life. By living in the present we enhance the joy of life itself. Most of our energy must be focused on the now, the moment we currently occupy, in order to make it the best it can be.

A good illustration of this is the old tale of the knight and the dragon. A knight is being chased by a fire breathing dragon. His horse is running full tilt, but the dragon is slowly gaining on him. Suddenly a great chasm appears before the knight. It is a mile across and several miles long. With the chasm before him and the fire breathing dragon behind, the knight brings his horse to an abrupt stop. Running to the chasm's edge, he looks down and sees a branch growing five feet below out of the side of the chasm. Feeling the heat from the dragon on his back, in desperation the knight leaps down and clutches the branch. Huge dragon above, nothingness below, for the moment he is safe. Then he notices a sound . . . a gnawing sound. Where the tree is growing out of the side of the chasm, there are rats chewing away at the branch. With his life to end in a moment, the knight catches sight of a big, ripe, luscious strawberry growing from a plant clinging to the side of the gigantic hole. Holding onto the branch with one hand, with the other he calmly plucks the strawberry and savors every bite.

Abraham Lincoln was purported to have said, "Most people are about as happy as they make up their minds to be." My friend Linda made up her mind that she was not going to live the rest of her life in misery over all the tragedy that had visited her. She decided to look for and eat all the delicious strawberries she could find. In the Declaration of Independence "the pursuit of happiness" was one of the inalienable rights included in its text. We must not only pursue happiness but must even claim it for our lives. Christ said, "I came that they might have life and have it abundantly." (John 10:10) To have an abundant, happy life is God's desire for our lives. Why not make it our priority as well?

Much in life is not good or bad in itself. We choose to view it as good or bad. To a large degree we can make ourselves unhappy by choosing to judge something that is intrinsically neutral as bad. I believe some people are happiest when they are unhappy. They are always looking for the down side in just about everything. Try your best to avoid these kinds of people. Do not allow them to pull you down with them. Life is too short to be spent around negative people. Join in the glee of a young child who eats ice cream for the first time. Freely laugh at yourself even when you say something stupid.

When we view our lives, like the proverbial glass, we see them either as half empty or half full. Take a rainy day for instance. One person sees rain as a blessing and another sees it as a nuisance because their hearts tell their minds what to see. But to a grateful heart, everything is a gift from God. Rain presents no problem for young children. Given the chance, my granddaughter would splash in every rain puddle she encountered. She celebrated rain and found glee in getting wet.

Years ago I led a tour that included a visit to Delphi, Greece. As we followed the guide up the hill of this ancient place and viewed the impressive archeological site, the day was clear and beautiful. By the time we walked all the way to the top of this marvelous spot, it began to rain. Before long the heavens opened wide with their bounty. Most of us did not have umbrellas. Those who did soon found that they were little help in the driving rain. We were all getting wet, and it was irritating all of us as we made our way for the half an hour walk back down the site to the bus.

Before long something began happening to all of us. We were all so soaked that it was impossible for us to get

any wetter. Water sloshed around in my shoes, for they were so wet. The ladies' eye mascara was making black streaks down their cheeks. Looking at one another, they began to laugh. We all began to be children once again having great fun at being completely wet. I closed my umbrella and began celebrating the experience.

Earlier in the day we decided to take a group picture with Delphi in the background. Looking somewhat ridiculous, we took the picture anyway. Ask any person on that tour, and they will tell you that this was one of the most memorable experiences on the entire tour. Everyone received a copy of the picture of their drenched selves to help them remember how much they all enjoyed this most special, rainy day.

We need to have an attitude of gratitude and choose to be happy every day. Make happiness a life priority. Life is not always easy. It is not always fair. Our happiness cannot be based on outward circumstances. It must come from within us. It is good to begin each day remembering that we have been claimed for eternity through the love manifested by God in Jesus Christ. This fact alone overflows our cup. Nearly everyone reading this book is not going to miss any meals soon. No one is homeless. Even those of us dealing with illness are blessed with medical care that can heal and extend our lives. And most of all, our God is as close to us as a whispered prayer- ready to help and to comfort and to console. How can we not be happy?

TWO

GOD MADE YOU AND GOD DOESN'T MAKE JUNK

On several occasions I have been privileged to take an African Safari. It was a wonderful experience like none other. Unlike a zoo, the animals roam free, and the safari traveler sits in a cage in the form of the safari vehicle. Not only are all of the animals magnificent, but the birds are unbelievably spectacular. They are multicolored and truly stunning. Many of the flowers are unique and vibrant, and the land itself is most interesting. The sunrises and sunsets are dramatic and beautiful. As the sun sets and the night sky comes into view, the senses are once again dazzled by thousands of stars.

But the most special thing I encountered on my safari were the African people. They were warm and welcoming. They were friendly and helpful. They were never too busy to stop what they were doing to assist you. Those who were Christians bubbled over with enthusiasm as they generously shared their faith with you. I went to Africa for the animals and birds and landscape but came home most impressed and touched by the people.

I should not have been surprised. For the most phenomenal thing created by God was people. When God made us, God may have declared, "another masterpiece like no other." There are no two of us alike. Even identical twins have their own unique personality. We are all one of a kind, an original, a signed masterpiece. The Bible tell us that we were made just a little lower than the angels. This is something worth feeling great about.

How do you feel about yourself? Are you in awe of yourself? Do you praise and thank God for creating you? You need to think and say, "I am loved by God, therefore I am blessed." Thinking positive thoughts leads to positive actions and feelings. Negative thoughts will rob you of joy and happiness. God created you on purpose. You are not an accident. You are especially made by God. In the over seven billion people on this planet, there is only one you. Never look down on yourself and focus on your flaws. Sure you have flaws. We all do. Rather focus on your specialness. Look at yourself with the eyes of God. Feel God's love for you. You are valuable to God. "How valuable?" Just look at Calvary's cross and the one who was crucified on it. That valuable.

Most of us would treasure owning an original painting by a famous artist. We would proudly hang it in a prominent place in our homes. When we look at ourselves in the mirror, do we not see reflected back the image of a person made by God? There is no better artist than God. In my travels when I visited old mansions, it was quite common to see the painted portraits of previous owners hanging in a prominent place in the house. Perhaps we as well should better celebrate God's spectacular work in creating us by having an equally large picture of us hanging conspicuously in our homes.

This morning when you combed your hair, did you count the number of hairs that ended up in your comb? Then did you subtract this number from the total number of hairs you had previously counted on your head? This then would result in you knowing the current count of all of the hairs on your head. Unless we were down to the last dozen or so hairs, this would be nearly impossible. You might not know the number, but God does. The Bible tells us that God is so interested in each of us, that God knows the number of hairs we each have on our heads. This is pretty amazing. Boy, God cares a lot about us to go even as far as to know the number of hairs on our heads.

God Doesn't Make Junk

Now if God values us so much, shouldn't we value ourselves as well? God made us, and God doesn't make any junk. There are times in our lives that most of us have feelings of inadequacy. Maybe we do not feel smart enough or lucky enough. There is always someone we know who is better looking than we are. There are friends with a nicer car or a bigger house. Childhood dreams of being a major league baseball player have now long vanished. We have found the corporate ladder too steep for us to make it to the top. In many ways, our lives have become a matter of settling. A dramatic improvement does not look promising. Currently, so many people are working very hard to just survive. The cost of living rises faster than their income. Most spouses are also working. There is less and less time available to be spent with their children and one another. This puts a strain on the family and on the marriage. Saving for the future and retirement is nearly impossible. Life is tenuous and hard at times. Abundance seldom visits. It is quite understandable that this daily reality makes many feel like junk.

For many of us, the lack of positive feelings of self-worth began when we were both very young and very impressionable. Someone who was a significant other in our lives one day told us that we were not nice looking or dumb or said something else negative. We took it to heart and many of us carried this negative feeling about ourselves into adulthood. I know the feeling well. Through high school and college, I do not remember ever getting an A on any writing assignment. I always considered myself just average in the writing department. Why would I think otherwise having been told this by many English teachers? What I did not realize was that writing was a late blooming talent in my life.

In a Moral Theology class I took at Union Seminary in New York City, we were told that our grade would be based on class participation and a term paper. Most of my class was made up of doctoral candidates who were very bright Jesuits already well versed in moral theology. I did not say one word during the entire semester, for I did not want to demonstrate my lack of knowledge in the subject matter. They probably all thought I was stupid, but had I opened my mouth, I would have removed all doubt.

At the end of the semester, everyone handed in their term papers. Most of my classmates wrote very lengthy, hernia producing papers. I turned in just five pages which reported the results of an original experiment I conducted. Two weeks later, I received a telephone call from the secretary of my professor who was also the Religious Education department chairperson. I was asked to come to his office to discuss my paper. As you might imagine, I was not feeling very good about my special invitation. He began by saying, "I hope that you do not mind Mr. Krahn, but I sent your paper to the editor of *Religious Education* for publication. I easily forgave him for not first asking my permission. From that day on, I no longer felt my writing was junk. Since then, I have been published over a hundred times. So when someone knocks you down, do not give up but get up. Do not let the comments of others define you, perhaps God is not finished with you yet. Although I am now retired, I have yet to be able to draw as well as a Fifth Grader, but I have not given up hope. Perhaps God has another surprise in store for me.

Made in the Image of God

The Bible tells us that we were made in the image of God. How could the image of God in any way be junk? In many ways, we are like God. We can think and can reason.

We can choose how we lead our lives. We are not programmed robots. We can create. God even left us in charge of all creation. It is in our power to either sustain it or destroy it. When God finished creating us, God admired us and said, "It is good." Nothing God made was more special or more beautiful than you and me. God not only didn't make any junk but couldn't make any junk. It is not in God's nature.

Sometimes our world puts too much value on youth and physical looks. In a famous Twilight Zone episode, we find a woman having plastic surgery to enhance her face because she was deemed so ugly. None of the faces of the characters were visible throughout the episode until the very end. Finally the bandages were removed from the poor lady's face. When she looked into the mirror, she screamed in disappointment. The operation was not successful. The camera first showed the woman's face as she saw herself in the mirror . . . it was actually gorgeous. Then the camera panned around the room at the doctors and nurses whose faces expressed horror and great disappointment at the outcome. All of their faces were ugly and grotesque. Beauty is in the eye of the beholder. God made every single face a beautiful face. Let me suggest that every morning when you get up and look in the mirror, say, "Hello good looking." Admire God's creation of you. Thank God for you just the beautiful way you are.

A woman is born with about two million eggs. She does not produce any more during her lifetime. Think how lucky you were to even be born. You beat two million to one odds and made it. We should never think of ourselves less than God thinks of us. So what if we have more or less hair. So what if we are too skinny (never a problem of mine). So what if we would never land a modeling contract. So what if we are not particularly athletic. We are here. We showed up in this world. That counts for a whole lot. What a great blessing this is in and of itself.

Most of us are blessed in great measure. We really have little to complain about. We are easily better off than 90% of our earth's inhabitants. But many of us find ourselves carping about a lot of things and looking for the junk in life rather than the blessings. A few people do this in the extreme. This is the way it was with Mrs. Krahm. She was one of my clients who I took on a tour of Israel and Egypt. From day one she was finding fault with the tour and complaining to anyone who would listen. Nothing seemed to satisfy her or make her happy. After a while, I noticed people avoiding her and her negative personality.

When we landed in Cairo Egypt, we stayed in a five star hotel beautifully located in an upscale neighborhood right on the Nile River. From the top floor, river side, one could see the Great Pyramids of Giza. It was pinch yourself perfect. My roommate was a bishop friend of mine who had invited Mrs. Krahm along. Entering our room, we noticed that there was only one large bed in the room. I called down to the desk to have our room changed. Since we were on the back side of the hotel, I was also hoping that we would wind up with a river view. Before long, the hotel manager was knocking on my room door. He was upset and told me that the hotel was completely booked without another available room. He had also made a big mistake.

Since my last name is *Krahn*, he had mistakenly put *Krahm* and her roommate in the penthouse suite that he had intended for the bishop and me. "I'll change it right away," he told me. "No you can't," I said, for I was certain that Mrs. Krahm and her roommate had already begun to unpack and luxuriate in their spectacular digs. Now I had been in this suite before. It was several rooms with the best view in the entire hotel of the Nile River and the pyramids. The penthouse suite had two separated bedrooms and bathrooms and a large living room. Included with the room was a bottle of wine, a fruit tray, and canapés. It was heaven on the Nile.

My friend, Bishop Rudy, and I would just have to make due in the standard room mistakenly given to us. We two men would even have to sleep together. I was literally in bed with the bishop. The next morning I saw Mrs. Krahm at breakfast. "How was your room?" I enthusiastically asked her. "Not bad," she replied, "but there was no stationery in the desk." True to form, she was not happy. Once again she focused upon the tiny piece of junk in the best of situations.

A friend of mine, who had earlier led a trip from Israel to Egypt, told me the story of their bus getting stuck in the sand that had blown across the road on their way through the Sinai desert. For the longest time, the driver tried to dislodge the bus, but all of his attempts failed. There was no bathroom on the bus, and many of the passengers were in much pain. In desperation, the wise Egyptian guide encouraged the passengers off the bus putting the women on one side of the bus and the men on the other in order to take care of their urgent personal needs. After the last passenger exited the bus, the driver tried once again to free the bus. This time he succeeded. And as the bus slowly pulled away, privacy for the men and women disappeared with it. Thankfully, Mrs. Krahm wasn't on this trip.

Much of the junk in our lives is produced by us. It comes with thinking less of ourselves than God thinks about us. It comes when we view our world through negative glasses. It emanates out of a bad attitude. It comes when we choose to be unhappy. It happens when we make bad choices in life. When temptation wins, junk rules. Trying to live life without God . . . junk. Waking up every day, head to the first mirror available, see your glorious self, and begin your day saying, "God made me and God doesn't make any junk." You might also wish to add, "God loves you, and I love you too."

Actually God wants more for us than we want for ourselves. God loves us more than we love ourselves. God wants us to be happy and fulfilled even more than we want it for ourselves. God created us with potential and wants us to reach it.   Success is what God wishes for our lives, not failure. And this will be ours when we welcome a fuller participation of God into our lives. Do not live one more day of your priceless life in a manner less than what God desires it to be.

When Jesus was born in Bethlehem, he was born the Son of God but also the Son of Man. Like us, he had two eyes, two hands, and two legs. There was nothing junky about Jesus. He was the beautiful Son of God and Son of Man. With the exception that Jesus was perfect and without sin, we are very much like him. And this is the problem. It is our sinful nature that brings much of the junk into our lives. With God's help, we must fight temptation and not fall into sin which pushes us away from God. And when we stay strong in our faith and love God deeply, we will not feel junky, and we will wind up living a much happier life.

THREE

ELIMINATE WORRY – THE JOY THIEF

I have been a clergy for nearly fifty years now. I have greeted well over a half million people at the end of nearly 5000 worship services which I have conducted. Not once in all these years, as people filed out of the church, did anyone say to me, "You know what pastor, I cheat on my taxes, or I beat my wife, or I steal from my employer?" But on any number of occasions, people said quite publically, "Pastor I am a worrier." They usually say this with a little smile on their faces. Most of us are so good at worrying that we do not realize that it is something God does not desire for our lives. Actually, it is against God's will for us to worry or to be fearful. Worry and fear are bed fellows. Someone has counted up in the Bible the number of times we are told not to fear, and it is over 365 times. This is once for every day in the year.

In the Bible we read, "Do not worry about anything." (Philippians 4:6) It can also be translated, "Have no anxiety about anything." Anxiety is a sadistic tyrant. It enslaves us and is one of the most negative parts of our existence. So we begin by asking ourselves, what is causing worry in our lives? How are we feeling anxious or fearful? None of these are happy feelings. They are happiness stealing thieves. Perhaps your employment is very tenuous. Maybe your teenagers are causing you worry, and you are concerned about their future. There is that little lump in your breast you just discovered that the doctor needs to check out. School exams are making you feel anxious. Will there be enough money to pay the bills at the end of the month? Some kids in school are picking on my kid. If all of this is not enough, reading or listening to the news can ruin anyone's day.

Good news seems to be in short supply these days. The political parties are always at odds. Some political figure or another is always heading to jail for corruption. There is one human tragedy after another taking place in our world. The economy is never as strong as we would like it to be. Someone is always murdering someone else. Many churches are struggling just to survive. Cancer still reigns as a major killer. Add to this the problems in our local states and communities, and there is a whole array of things worthy of worry. We could further enlarge all of these by our propensity to worry even when things are going relatively well in our lives. There is that general fear of tomorrow and what negative things it may bring to our lives.

There is no quick fix for worry and anxiety . . . no foolproof pill . . . no magic bullet. But there is good news; there is help available for us to cope with our worry and anxiety and the fear that often grips our lives. We can even defeat it. It is not easy. Once we are more effectively dealing with one worry, another often seems to pop up. As imperfect people prone to worry, we need to just keep on keeping on. We must make a conscious decision that we will not accept worry as a normal way of living and allow it to rob us of joy in our lives.

Worry Is a Sin

The first thing that I need to say right off the bat is that worry is a sin. We do not often see it as a sin because we are so good at it. There is so much good cause and reason to worry that it is hard to think of worrying as sinful. Not only does St. Paul say to the church in Philippi not to worry, but Jesus says in the Sermon on the Mount not to worry as well. In Matthew 6:25-34 we read Jesus' words:

> 25 Therefore I tell you, do not worry about your life, what you will eat or what you will drink, or about your body, what you will wear. Is not life more than food, and the body more than clothing? 26 Look at the birds of the air; they neither sow nor reap nor gather into barns, and yet your heavenly Father feeds them. Are you not of more value than they? 27 And can any of you by worrying add a single hour to your span of life? 28 And why do you worry about clothing? Consider the lilies of the field; they neither toil nor spin, 29 yet I tell you, even Solomon in all his glory was not clothed like one of these. 30 But if God so clothes the grass of the field, which is alive today and tomorrow is

thrown into the oven, will he not much more clothe you – you of little faith? 31 Therefore do not worry, saying, 'What will we eat?' or 'What will we drink?' or 'What will we wear?' 32 For it is the Gentiles who strive for all these things, and indeed your heavenly Father knows that you need all these things. 33 But strive first for the kingdom of God and his righteousness, and all these things will be given to you as well. 34 So do not worry about tomorrow, for tomorrow will bring worries of its own. Today's trouble is enough for today.

Jesus concludes his teaching on worry by stating that we are not to worry a bit about tomorrow. Let today's trouble be enough for us today. Do not worry about tomorrow. We either trust that God's help is there for us for both today and tomorrow or we don't. One day at a time Jesus teaches. Otherwise we add to today's burden the weight of tomorrow's burden as well. We are sapping more joy from today by also worrying about the future.

Worry is a sin that consumes our joy and steals our happiness. Worry is a life destroying disease. We hate it. And God hates it even more. If we are not willing to trust the Lord with our worries, we are saying, "Lord, I am smarter than you. I am more capable than you. You are not up to the challenge that my problems pose." How foolish this is. Worry is actually an insult to God. Those of us who attend church and receive Holy Communion receive God's forgiveness and eternal salvation. If we are willing to trust God with our eternal future, we can surely trust God with our temporal problems. God wishes to be involved with us both in our todays as well as in our eternal tomorrows.

Fear and worry are twin foes of the human soul. They are deadly enemies of faith. Faith and worry are never happy companions. It is hard to have them both at the same time. One displaces the other as surely as water displaces air when it fills a glass. We cannot be trusting in the Lord fully at the same time we are filled with anxiety. Faith and trust displace worry and fear when we allow them to flood our lives. Martin Luther once wrote, "Pray and let God worry." Thanksgiving and rejoicing are the sure signs that faith and trust are dominant in our lives. The bigger we magnify God in our lives, the smaller our problems become.

Years ago before cell phones, a friend of mine told me the story of a weekend her daughter went skiing with some of her friends. My friend lived on Long Island, and the daughter went skiing in upstate New York about a four hour drive away. As my friend and her husband were getting ready to visit friends on Sunday night, she received a telephone call from her daughter. Snow was starting to fall, and it was predicted that it would become severe. They were starting for home early hoping to get back to Long Island before too much accumulated on the roads. "Don't worry if I arrive home late," she told her mother.

The mother told her daughter everything any mother would tell her daughter. "Be careful . . . drive slowly . . . if road conditions get too bad, find a motel and stay over . . . and by all means, let me know if you do." Throughout the entire evening with friends, the mother's mind kept seeing the daughter driving at night under poor conditions. Finally, she and her husband arrived home just before midnight. She knew she couldn't sleep, so she would wait up until her child arrived home safe and sound. It became 1 a.m., and no daughter; 2 a.m. no daughter; 4 a.m. and still no daughter. The mother was becoming increasingly frantic. She listened to the news to see if there was any report of an accident. She wondered whether she should call and wake up the parents of her daughter's friends; perhaps their children had called and informed their parents. The sleepless, painful, worry filled night dragged on.

Around 7 a.m., my friend hears a sound coming from her daughter's upstairs room. Moments later, the daughter comes down the steps into the living room where her mother had been camped out all night. The bad snow had not materialized. They had gotten home in record time. She put her stuff away and did not leave it lying around the living room as she normally did. She decided not to have her usual cup of bedtime tea and leave her cup in the sink. She went right to bed just before her parents returned home from their friend's house. The mother lovingly told me that when she saw her daughter bounding down the stairs, "I could have killed her."

All night her daughter was safe at home and upstairs sleeping in her own bed while her mother was consumed with worry downstairs. We can all relate to my friend's dilemma, for we have all needlessly worried many times in our lives. When Mark Twain was an old man, he purportedly said that if he had known that most of what he worried about during his lifetime never came to fruition, he would not have worried so much.

Rejoice in All Things

Rejoice in all things, rejoice and live a life having no anxiety about anything, Paul encourages us. "Anything St. Paul?" we may be tempted to say. "You have got to be kidding me. Did you see my current set of monthly bills? Are you aware of the deteriorating physical condition of my mother? Have you seen me lately before I put on my makeup? Do you know that I need another car but cannot afford one? How can you say such words? What right have you to even write such things?"

St. Paul might just respond to our challenge of his words in this way, "Have you been struck blind for three days because you persecuted the Lord's followers? Has your life ever been threatened by an angry mob? Have you been attacked and beaten and thrown into prison not because you committed a crime but because you were sharing your love for the Lord? Have you ever had forty men take an oath that they would not eat or drink until they killed you? Have you languished for years in a prison that was nothing more than a hole in the ground lacking even the most basic necessities?" Many scholars believe that Paul was in such a prison in Rome when he wrote his letter to the Philippian Christians. I once visited the first century prison in Rome believed to be the very prison in which St. Paul was placed for years before he was finally martyred. Basically it was a large hole. We got to climb down inside of it. On one of the walls of the hole, there was a piece of wood which covered an opening in the wall. I asked the guide what was the wood covering. She said it was an entrance into the ancient sewage system of Rome. I could readily imagine the filth and stench and rats which Paul had to contend with daily. If there was ever a person who earned the right to say to me, "John, rejoice in your life; rejoice in your problems; rejoice in your challenges, and rejoice in everything" . . . this person was St. Paul.

The early Christians counted suffering for Christ not as a burden or misfortune but as a great honor and blessing. In their suffering, they felt that they could better bear witness to their love of their Lord. They literally rejoiced in all things. Tacitus, a Roman historian, wrote about the early Christian martyrs. He told how they were covered with skins of beasts and torn apart by dogs. They were crucified. At night they were burned for illumination. Nero offered his gardens for the spectacle. The martyrs went rejoicing to their deaths, as if they were going to a marriage feast. They marched into the arena as if marching into heaven. When

St. Ignatius, an early martyr, was about to die for his faith in 110 A.D., he courageously cried out, "Nearer the sword, then nearer to God. In company with wild beasts, in company with God."

After being encouraged to rejoice in all things and have no anxiety about anything, Paul tells us with prayer and thanksgiving to make our requests known to God. And when we do this, St. Paul promises us that we will receive what he did in his life. Trusting in the Lord in all things and laying our concerns at his feet, we receive a wonderful gift. That gift is none other than the riches of God's peace and along with it happiness and joy. Peace of mind and heart is one of the best gifts given to us by God this side of eternity. Now peace is not a place where there is no trouble. It is a place within us where we can go during trouble and find calm in our heart.

English poet, Elizabeth Cheney, writes of an imaginary conversation between two birds observing the human race while perched in the top of a tree. The two birds speak to one another.

"Said the Robin to the Sparrow,
'I should really like to know,
Why these anxious human beings
Rush around and worry so.'"

"Said the Sparrow to the Robin,
'Friend I think it must be
That they have no heavenly Father
Such as cares for you and me.'"

But we do. We certainly do. We have a God that cares for us much more than the sparrow and the robin. God even allowed Jesus to be impaled on a cross for our sake. There is no greater love and caring than this. Trust in the Lord. Trust in God with your entire being. And God will cast out all of your fears and your anxieties and worries and will replace them with heavenly peace.

The story is told of the old, wise family doctor who tells his patients to say their prayers and then add, "Goodnight worries, see you in the morning." This is pretty good advice. But I might suggest one better, "Goodnight worries, no need for you in my life, for I have cast all my worries on the Lord who cares for me."

FOUR

EFFECTIVELY DEALING WITH LIFE'S HURTS

I live on Long Island in New York. Most of the workers who commute daily to the city take the Long Island Railroad. One day a nice woman, who rides the train daily, noticed a disheveled old man sitting one seat ahead of her. He was dressed poorly and looked down on his luck. Feeling sorry for him, the lady reached into her purse, took out a twenty dollar bill, walked over to the man, and in an act of Christian charity placed the bill into his hand and said, "Sir, never despair, always remember, never despair."

The next day, taking the identical train to work, the woman noticed when the same old man boarded her train. He immediately walked over to her, and to her great surprise, he placed a hundred dollar bill into her hands. Startled, she asked the fellow, "Why are you doing this?" He responded, "Never Despair won the sixth race at Belmont Raceway and paid five to one."

Although this story is cute, there is nothing cute about feelings of despair. Unfortunately, at one time or another we have all felt them. Everyone who has a few years under the belt has experienced his or her share of life's hurts. Some of these hurts are quite traumatic like losing a loved one or seeing a marriage dissolve. Other hurts include not reaching our life's goals, facing the reality of aging with its limitations, or discovering that we have lost all of our ability to communicate with someone we love. Unresolved feelings of hurt rob us of the joy of living. If we look to live a better, more enriching life, we need to find out how to better live with our hurts or better yet, to overcome them.

At the center of dealing with life's hurts is a life centered on Jesus Christ. A casual relationship with the Lord may help us weather small problems, but a major hurt needs to be able to draw upon a deep well of faith that has been nurtured by frequent prayer, regular worship, and a knowledge of the Bible.

Jesus said that he came into the world so that we could be blessed with an abundant life. Yes, the abundance of eternity, but also with a happy and fulfilling daily life as well. An abundant life results from an abundance of Christ in our lives.

Years ago I had to meet with the president of our small, local bank to try to arrange a short term loan for our church. During our conversation, I inquired whether he attended a church in the area. He told me, "Not regularly, for I believe there is such a thing as having too much religion." I then asked him if he could imagine a time when his bank would make too much money, and he would consequently have to close it several days a week to keep the profits down? He quickly responded that he could not envision such a scenario. I told him that in like manner I could not conceive of my receiving too much of God's abundance in my life. We especially need such abundance to draw upon when life hurts us badly.

In my last year of seminary, one of my classmates was hit head-on while driving home from conducting services at a local, country church. His pregnant wife was killed outright along with their baby. He was left in a coma. She was a Lutheran school teacher. The church where she taught was packed for her funeral. He was not even able to attend. It was one of the saddest occasions in my life that I can ever remember. Everyone present was devastated. During his sermon, the pastor of the church said that she was now in a better place having left the veil of tears of this life. Not once did he acknowledge the tragic circumstances of her death but glossed over it with one religious cliché after another. I was so angry. I felt like screaming, "You've got to be kidding, for this was perhaps the happiest moment in her life. Her husband was just a few weeks away from receiving his first call as pastor of a church. They were both awaiting the joy of their first child . . . veil of tears, what veil of tears?"

Our Seminary President was then given the opportunity to say a few words. Dr. Alfred Fuerbringer had many gifts, but preaching was not among them. Yet on that day of terrible hurt, the hand of God was clearly upon him.

He spoke, "We have all experienced a terrible loss. A young woman in the prime of her life is gone. Her unborn child also gone. And her husband cannot even be here at their funeral, for he remains in critical condition in the hospital. We cannot begin to understand why this happened. But this we know . . . God is here with us in our hurt. And through our tears and with faith we proclaim that she is in a better place. We find comfort in this even as we grieve such a senseless loss." I felt like applauding and hugging him.

At times of tragedy, we are all prone to ask the question, "Where is God in the whole mess of living?" I believe that God is the still point in a turning, chaotic world. Our God is present bringing calm out of chaos. God is a source of hope in the face of despair. With God's help we can even snatch victory from the jaws of defeat.

Life Is Not Fair

To successfully cope with life's hurts, we must begin by honestly telling it as it is. Life is both not fair and unjust. At times life can seem lousy. But God is not the author of tragedy whether it be for a seminarian couple or for anyone else. God did not pilot the two planes into the Twin Towers. Our God does not inflict cancer on any one. The insurance company speaks of certain tragic events like tornados that wipe out towns and take lives as, "Acts of God." This is a most unfortunate misnomer. God never brings hurt and tragic death to our doorstep. But God is *actively* there with us at those moments bringing comfort and help.

Having honestly acknowledged our hurt, we let God take hold of our hand remembering God's comforting words that we should not fear. God is always present to help and comfort us. God does not say, "I will do it all for you," but "I will help you." We have all been blessed by God with certain abilities. We first ask God to help us use the abilities we have. If we are momentarily lacking confidence, we lean on God as we move forward together. The Bible assures us that we can do all things with Christ who strengthens us. Believing this, we step out in faith. We do not know what lies ahead, but we know that the God of our present is also the God of our future.

In biblical times, after a man carried a heavy burden for a prescribed distance, he would not put it down on the ground for the next person to pick up. Rather he would roll it from his shoulders onto the shoulders of the next person who would carry it. Likewise we need to roll our problems and hurts from our shoulders to the waiting and willing shoulders of our Lord Jesus Christ.

The Healing Power of Enthusiasm

When we are hurting, being enthusiastic seems almost absurd. In the beginning of the book of Acts, we read how Peter and the apostles were flogged for preaching the

Gospel. Later in Acts, we read of Paul and Silas being beaten by rods and thrown into prison. In both cases these men rejoiced that they could suffer for the sake of the gospel. The word *enthusiasm* is comprised of two Greek words, *en theos.* Translated the words mean, "In God." These men were enthusiastic, for their lives were entwined with God's. They had the presence and inspiration of God helping them to meet the hurts and challenges of each new day. The reality and power of the risen Christ was theirs. Neither the pain of beatings, the disgrace of imprisonment, nor the fear of death was allowed to dampen their enthusiasm for their ministry.

Even when we are hurting, meaningful life is possible when we are *en theos.* The art of developing a happy, enthusiastic, and meaningful life develops as we allow Jesus Christ to soak into our hearts by meditating on his Word and being an active part of his church while regularly receiving the Sacraments. We need to invite God's life-changing presence to remake our negative attitudes into positive ones and to give us renewed energy for life and living. This happens as we realize that our lives are not an entitlement but a gift from God to be lived enthusiastically.

The Rev. Dr. Norman Vincent Peale tells the story of a surgeon friend. Dr. Peale asked the doctor, "What's the most exciting operation you have ever performed in your entire life?" Thinking for a moment, the doctor replied,

You know, of all the surgeries that I've performed, there is one that stands out that changed my life. There was a little girl with only a ten percent chance that she would survive. When I went into the operating room, there she was, a tiny little thing under the sheet, ashen grey face, so frail, so weak and helpless. I walked up to her, and she looked at me and said, 'May I say something, doctor?' I said, 'Sure, honey.' 'Well,' she said, 'every night before I go to sleep I always say a prayer. May I pray a prayer now?' I said, 'Of course.' Now I was having troubles of my own with my son and in my home. And I had become a very unhappy person. So I said, 'Sure, honey, you pray and you pray for your doctor too.' Then she prayed the prayer, 'Jesus tender Shepherd hear me. Watch your little lamb tonight. Through the darkness be Thou near me, keep me safe 'til morning light. And Jesus, bless the doctor, because he has troubles too.'

It just broke me up. As I was washing up, I prayed like I had never prayed before and said, 'Oh God, in my whole life if you ever use me to save a life, use me now to save this little girl.' A miracle happened. The surgery was a success, and her life was saved. When I got dressed and left, I felt that I also had an operation that morning. I had Jesus put into me!

When we are hurting, we need to have the healing power of Jesus put into us. Then we can better live our lives enthusiastically . . . in God.

Three Ways God Helps Us

In summary, God helps us in three ways. First, "God helps those who help themselves." How often have we heard this spoken? But it is true. I have already spoken that God gives us tools and abilities that we can use to help our situation. Soon after his surgery, a car accident patient who had severe injuries to his spine asked his doctor, "Do you think I will be able to walk again?" With gentleness the doctor answered, "There is a more important question you need to be asking. It is this. Do you believe you will be able to walk again?" When we have problems we either flee from God or flee to God. Believe always that with God's help all things are possible.

Next, God helps us through other people. Let your family and friends know that you are hurting. God touches you through the lives of these special people in your life. Your church family is also a ready resource God uses. Everyone has experienced moments of need in their lives. There is nothing to be embarrassed about. When you reach out to others, they will understand and not think less of you.

A famous painter decided one day to paint a picture of the church. He painted a boat in trouble in a stormy sea. Black ominous clouds graced the top of the painting. Huge waves had just caused the boat to sink. All hands were overboard. Several sailors had reached a large rock sticking out of the water and were clinging to it with both hands. Others were still struggling to reach it. At first the painter was pleased with the painting and its symbolism. The rock was the church, and it provided salvation for troubled souls. But the more he considered his painting, the unhappier he became with it.

He decided to start afresh. In his second painting, there was the same ferocious storm at sea, the capsized boat, all hands overboard, the rock of salvation, some men reaching it while others still struggling to do so. But in his second painting, the men having reached the safety of the rock were holding onto it with only one hand. With their other hand, they were reaching out trying to save their drowning brothers. Allow your church to reach out to you in your time of need.

Several years ago at a Special Olympics track meet, six kids lined up to race. The gun sounded. Half way to the finish line, the child leading the race tripped somehow and fell sprawling face first on the track. Seeing this, the other five competitors did something that made this race like no other. They stopped, went to the hurt child, helped him up, and arm in arm they all ran together crossing the finish line as one. Touched by such a generous spirit, the judges awarded six gold medals for this special event . . . one to each runner. God helps us through the good hearts of other people.

Finally God helps us directly. "Heaven help me," we sometimes say in a moment of anguish. And the God of heaven does. Through prayer, God sends guidance, comfort, and the help we need to cope and heal. Miracles continue to happen and come from the loving heart of God. I believe in miracles; I have observed them often in my long ministry. Tap directly into the power and the wisdom and the love of God. We also must not allow ourselves to become despondent. We need to keep a strong PMA . . . i.e. Positive Mental Attitude. There is no room for negative thinking, for we have God on our side.

It is a true fact of the American Revolution that George Washington and the American army lost almost every battle they fought against the vastly superior British army. At that time, Great Britain was the mightiest nation on earth. We won the American Revolution not by winning battles but by tenacity. We didn't surrender to our enemy. Knocked down, we got up. Beaten, we continued to fight. We won because we simply refused to lose. Whatever your life challenges are, however bleak the situation seems, however much you are hurting, do not give up. God is on your side.

Every day is a gift from God to be lived to its fullest. We get only one opportunity to live today . . . so why not live it to its fullest? In our life, we find our refuge and strength in God. With confidence we proclaim, "My hope is built on nothing less than Jesus' blood and righteousness. . . . On Christ, the solid rock I stand, all other ground is sinking sand." We can effectively deal with life's hurts. Even better, we can have victory over them.

FIVE

THE WHY OF SUFFERING

God does not sit up in heaven and decide who to inflict with cancer and who to give a pass. God does not select a young child to die tragically in a fire. God does not break up marriages. God does not incite genocide. God does not play favorites and love some people more than others. God takes no pleasure in suffering, and God does not cause suffering. If God did, I would not believe in such a God and would not be writing this book. Our God is a loving God who does not arbitrarily cause suffering.

So what is the source of suffering? Much of it comes from poor decisions we make. Drive too fast, get into an accident and suffer. Smoke, get lung cancer and suffer. Fail to put in a smoke detector, there is a fire, and people suffer. Steal, go to jail and suffer. Neglect our family, it breaks apart, and we suffer. Most of suffering is the result of sin.

Suffering also results from bad decisions other people make. Someone runs a red light; we are hit, and we wind up in the hospital if not the funeral home. Our leaders make decisions based upon what is good for them rather than what is good for the country, and many people suffer as a result. Parents indulge their children too much, and they turn out poorly, and both parents and their children suffer. Teachers and clergy do not take the time to prepare and be the best they can be, and those who depend on them suffer.

Suffering is also the result of evil. Six million Jews exterminated . . . evil. War in Syria . . . evil. Religious intolerance leading to religious persecution . . . evil. Racial intolerance . . . evil. Flying two airplanes into the Twin Towers . . . evil. Corporate greed which often brings suffering to those who are underpaid . . . evil. Those with plenty who neglect the poor . . . evil.

Floods, tornadoes, hurricanes, wild fires, drought, and other natural occurrences can cause much suffering as well. Are these acts of God? I do not believe so. These are all aspects of nature that are part of the world we inhabit. If I choose to live in a flood zone, and my house gets flooded, is this God's fault? If lightning or a careless camper causes a wild fire that destroys hundreds of homes, do we lay this suffering at God's feet? If people die of starvation because of a drought in Africa while other parts of the world have plenty but fail to share it with those who are suffering, do we blame God? If I live in tornado alley but have not provided a safe place for my family, aren't I to blame if we suffer injury?

When we ask the question of "why suffering," we must first remember that we are not in heaven yet. There is no suffering in heaven. Cancer is locked out of heaven. Broken relationships are not allowed in heaven. No need for hospitals in heaven. The funeral business is out of business in heaven. War . . . not allowed. Famine also not allowed. Poverty gone. Police in heaven, yes but out of a job. Until we get to heaven, suffering unfortunately will be with us.

The Suffering of J.B

In 1958, Archibald MacLeish published his Pulitzer Prize winning drama *J.B.* It retold the story of the Biblical figure Job in the person of a twentieth century American, millionaire banker named J.B. God allows J.B. to be stripped of his family and wealth, yet he refuses to turn his back on God. *J.B* brought a modern and powerful recast of the Biblical account.

J.B. is a happy man with a lovely wife and children. He is virtuous and respected. He has great wealth and power. Like Job, he was nearly perfect and upright and loved God and hated evil. He was one of a kind. That's our J.B. And from him everything he treasured in life was taken. Life hurts him in every way it possibly could. It starts with two soldiers knocking on his door. The war, just over, had brought the family hope of the safe return of their son David. There was the foolish skirmish, and David their eldest was dead. The news from the soldiers hit J.B and his wife Sarah hard.

Not long after the loss of their first born, on their way home from the Opera, our still grieving couple were greeted by the press. They came seeking a picture of devastated parents having just learned that two of their other children were killed in a car accident caused by a drunken, teenage driver. The press got its picture. Now only one child left, Ruth, and the explosion took her along with J.B's bank and fortune. David, Jonathan, Mary, Ruth, gone . . . all four of his precious children ripped from his heart.

And through all of his pain, J.B. still is able to say, "The Lord giveth, and the Lord taketh . . . " And Sarah, his wife, screams, "takes, no kills, kills, kills." Struggling on, J.B. somehow is able to continue, "Blessed be the name of the Lord." But unfortunately this isn't the end of poor J.B's suffering. You will recall the boils. His body is encrusted with sores, and pain is his constant companion. Seeing her husband deranged by grief, nauseated by the foul smell of his own flesh, and having become the modern definition of suffering, Sarah his wife, cries out to him, "Curse God, J.B., curse God and die." Refusing still to curse God, J.B. dissolves before the question, "Why . . . why me God?"

Whether in the Biblical story of Job or the modern retelling of it in *J.B.* all of us find ourselves there in the story somewhere. Whenever suffering invades our lives and we ask, "Why God, why me?" are we not being somewhat self-righteous? To ask, "Why me?" sees no purpose in suffering and suggests that we are so good that we do not deserve to suffer. Could we not better ask, "Why not me?" Only Jesus, the perfect one, could rightly ask, "My God, my God, why hast thou forsaken me?" I am not suggesting that the amount of suffering in our lives equates with the amount of our sinfulness. But suffering is often a regular part of everyone's life.

The Positive Side of Suffering

Who among us has recently prayed, "Almighty God, things have been going so well of late. I just got a promotion at work. Everyone likes me. My health has never been better. And I just won a million dollars in the lottery. Dear Lord, please allow some suffering to come my way, for with all of the recent good fortune, I am feeling very self-centered and smug. Sadly, I find myself so caught up in my good fortune, that you God are becoming less in my life. Dear Lord, please allow Satan to inflict me with some suffering." I doubt if any of us has ever or will ever pray such a prayer. It is not in our nature. We do pray that God removes suffering from our lives.

When St. Paul wrote his second letter to the Christians at Corinth, he was suffering. The exact nature of his illness is never mentioned, but the pain seemed to be daily and persistent. It was such that Paul pleads with God not just once, not even twice, but three times that God would give him relief from his pain. He even wonders why God allows this "Messenger of Satan," as he calls it, to remain and constantly hurt him.

Paul connects his suffering to a privilege which he earlier experienced in which he had a vision of being in heaven and experiencing God in a spectacular manner. This is something of which he could easily boast. He could even boast that on the road to Damascus he was converted by none other than Jesus. Then he was personally selected by our Savior Jesus himself to share the good news of his resurrection. Paul's conversion could have left him so puffed up with himself that he would have become useless to God.

Paul's illness was the natural result of his sinful, fallen nature. "Why am I suffering so?" Paul may have nevertheless wondered. "Why me?" Wasn't Paul a dynamic servant of God? Didn't Jesus hand pick him to share the Good News to the Gentiles? Wasn't Paul to eventually become the most influential follower of Christ who ever lived? "Come on God, this is Paul begging you now for the third time to pull this painful thorn out of my side." I am sure that Paul stayed up nights wondering why God wasn't answering his prayers. The pain remained. Was God asleep? Didn't God care?

Finally, after God ignored Paul's third request that the suffering end, Paul realized that God was in fact answering his prayer. The prayer was not being answered as Paul wanted it answered but as he needed it answered. By allowing him to continue to suffer, God was telling Paul that God's grace was enough for him and that God's power was made perfect in weakness. Paul is told that God's strength is more powerfully his when he is weak. "Do I understand this correctly?" Paul must have wondered, "Is

God blessing my life by allowing me to continue suffering?" Through suffering Paul was drawn closer to God, relied more on God, was less prone to become boastful, and drew from God a power much greater than he himself possessed. Paul eventually came to see his suffering as a blessing.

In Chapter Three of this book, we saw how the first century Christian martyrs suffered and made a powerful witness of their faith in God. Their willingness to suffer and be killed continues to witness to the church even down until today. During the Second World War, Dietrich Bonhoeffer became another Christian martyr whose death continues to be a powerful witness today. Bonhoeffer could have remained in the safety of the United States but instead returned to his native country of Germany to speak out against the evil Third Reich. Both his book, *The Cost of Discipleship,* and more importantly the witness of his life demonstrated how God can use suffering and even death for good.

God reminds Paul that the grace he has received is sufficient for him. This grace was not cheap grace, as Bonhoeffer points out in his book, but costly, for it became ours through the suffering and death of Jesus Christ at Golgotha. Even Jesus prayed the cup of suffering be removed from him. When it was not, Jesus submitted himself to the will of God and continued on his way to the cross.

When we are suffering, and we ask God to heal us and the suffering continues, might God be answering our prayer in a similar manner that God answered that of St. Paul? Maybe it is not the answer we want but a positive answer nevertheless. Could God even use our suffering to some good effect in our lives? Is there a blessing in our suffering somewhere of which we are currently unaware? Believers do not allow the negatives in their lives to draw them away from God but closer to God. Rather than asking God, "Why," perhaps the better question is "What." What Lord do you want to teach me through my suffering?

Suffering is an aspect of everyone's life, nothing anyone wants, nothing we would ever pray for, but like St. Paul, something we need to accept. When our suffering continues, we try to find something positive in it and try to understand why God allows it to continue. We allow it to draw us even closer to God while asking God's help in bearing it. When Paul writes to the church in Rome, he says that all things can work together for good to God's glory. This even includes suffering.

God Responds to Elijah's Suffering

We remember the story of Elijah and his contest with the prophets of Baal on Mount Carmel. After God gave Elijah a great and dramatic victory over them, Elijah killed them. When Jezebel, the wicked queen, heard that her prophets were all slain by Elijah, she was angry. She sent a message to Elijah that she would kill him. Afraid, Elijah fled for his life. He was suffering so much anguish that he even asked God to allow him to die. In response to his prayer, God sent Elijah an angel who gave him food and drink. The food provided supernatural strength for his long journey to Horeb, the mountain of God. There Elijah met the Lord. Elijah had nursed his suffering and depression into a pity party. He was running away from life itself. And what does God do? God sustains Elijah and then sends him back to work doing the Lord's bidding.

Now God was not the source of Elijah's suffering. It was evil Ahab and Jezebel. But God was there for Elijah in his suffering. God is there for us as well even when all we want to do is run away from our lives. That is the kind of God we have . . . one that does not cause suffering but is there for us when we are hit by it. So both in times of good health and plenty as well as in times of suffering and scarcity, we can rightly sing, "Praise God, from whom all blessings flow; Praise him all creatures here below; Praise him above ye heav'nly hosts; Praise Father, Son, and Holy Ghost."

SIX

LIVING LIFE AT ITS HIGHEST LEVEL

"I will live today as if it is my last." Write it down. What? These words, "I will live today as if it is my last." Paste it on your refrigerator door. What? These words, "I will live today as if it is my last." Memorize it. What? These words, "I will live today as if it is my last." Upon waking up in the morning, say your prayers and after the "Amen," say out loud, "This is the day the Lord has made, I will rejoice and be glad in it. And I will live today as if it is my last."

When my children were young, we bought a gerbil for them. It lived in a big, glass tank on top of the clothes dryer in the laundry room which also served as my little office. To give the poor creature a chance to exercise, we put a little wheel inside his tank so that he could run. He would get on that wheel and run as fast as he could. He then hopped off, looked around a bit, got back on and ran some more. I often wondered what he thought. I'd muse that the gerbil felt that running on the wheel would get him out of the tank to a better place. Upon running his little heart out, then hopping off the wheel, did he think, "Ah shucks, I'm still stuck in this stinking tank?"

Sometimes our lives are like that of my gerbil. We run around all day doing the same old thing and enjoy it about as much as the gerbil on the exercise wheel. We get stuck in a mindless routine, and one day blends into another that blends into yet another. We remain in the same old stinking tank of our routine and uninspiring lives. We are living our lives not even approaching the highest level.

C.S. Lewis, the famous Christian writer, once asked the question, "Where is the life we have lost in living?" One day we may wake up and lament that we took too much of our life for granted and did not do the things that we now wish we would have done. Our lives having been lost in the routine of mindless living . . . wasted endlessly on our cell phones or watching T.V. This in itself is not bad, but we could have used some of those hours doing something much better.

Your Money or Your Life?

The comic Jack Benny told the story that a robber walked up to him pointing a gun at his stomach and said, "your money or your life?" Benny doesn't answer right away. Irritated, the robber says a second time in a much louder voice, "Mister, your money, or your life?" Benny responds, "Patience, I'm thinking, I'm thinking." "Money or your life" is really a decision that all of us make every day. For most of us, if we want more money we need to work longer hours. Many of us even work two jobs allocating a greater amount of our available time for making money. We have come to believe that the more money we earn the better and happier our lives become. But is that necessarily the case? The truth of the matter is, the more hours we spend working, the fewer we have available to do other things. Everyone gets just 168 hours every week. None get more; none get less. We need to make a conscious decision how we will use them.

If we spend less money, the need to earn more money becomes unnecessary. Perhaps we could ditch the second job or not do the overtime if we changed our spending habits. Let me give some examples. There is nothing wrong with eating out. It is very enjoyable. Let's say a nice dinner for two at a restaurant comes to $80.00. If you are working four hours at the second job for $20.00 an hour, then four hours of time working would be needed to provide for just that meal. We need to ask ourselves, what is more important, four hours home with our family or the restaurant dinner? If the dinner were to celebrate one's anniversary, perhaps the dinner would be the better choice. At other times, it probably is not. But when it comes to having the latest iPhone or a new car rather than a used one and considering the hours of work needed to have the more expensive thing, perhaps more quality time at home with our children and spouse is the better choice for a happier life.

Some financial writers have suggested that we consider how many hours of work is needed for everything we purchase. This includes the stop at Starbucks, buying lunch out rather than bringing a sack lunch to work, going to the movies rather than renting one at home, and buying more clothes when the old ones can be worn much longer.

It also includes impulse buying of any kind or paying list price for something rather than seeking a discount. These are just a few of many examples. The object of this exercise is not to make our life boring but to make it better by making a conscious decision to get more bang for our buck so that we need fewer of them. This then results in having more time to enjoy a more meaningful life. Remember, we have just 168 hours per week. We have no power to increase that number. We do have the ability to decide how to make the most out of them.

A Life Lesson from Mike and Fran

Sometime back I read a poignant piece in the New York Times about a rising comic by the name of Mike DeStefano who died of a heart attack at age 44. He was a native of the Bronx, lived a tough life, was once hooked on heroin, and at the time of the article was H.I.V. positive. His girlfriend, Fran, had also been a junky and like him, was H.I.V. positive as well. Not knowing how long either of them would live, they moved to Florida expecting to die like the old people there. After about five years, his girlfriend, now wife, got very sick and was clearly dying. During Fran's last days while she was in hospice care, Mike got a motorcycle. Showing her his new Harley, Fran got very upset at him. She felt that he was moving on with his life while she was dying. Now that he had the motorcycle, she felt like he didn't need her anymore.

Calmed down, the next day Fran asked Mike to let her see his Harley once again. He took her out to see it. She asked to sit on it. Then she asked him to start it up. She was wearing a paper, hospital gown and holding her IV drip pole, and Mike worried that she might catch fire. With a pleading voice she asks him, "Can you take me for a little ride around the parking lot?" Afraid that she might fall off and kill herself, Mike wanted to say no, but they were in the moment, and he felt that he had to give her a ride.

He slowly rode her around the parking lot, while she held the I.V. morphine drip on a pole with four, little wheels attached to the bottom. They were clanging loudly. As they passed the front door of the hospice, soon a group of nurses came out and were watching this unusual sight. The nurses began to cry. At the time, Mike didn't realize why because he was so into pleasing his dying wife. She was once a prostitute and beaten by pimps. She was a heroin addict and now ends up with AIDS. Dying, all she wants is a ride on his new motorcycle. If this is what she wanted, Mike was not going to deny her.

The parking lot was not enough; Fran wanted to fully experience the Harley. Ditching the pole that holds her I.V., they took off. Holding the morphine bag over her head, before long they are flying down I 95 with Fran's paper dress flying up exposing her naked and emaciated body. Mike and Fran were lost in the moment and living their lives at the highest level. Fran died shortly after the Harley ride. It was the last thing her husband did with her. Looking back on this special moment, Mike felt that marrying Fran was the greatest decision he ever made and taking care of his wife was the greatest thing that he ever did. With their crazy motorcycle ride, Mike and Fran showed us all how to live even when staring death in the face.

Live the Fullest Life Possible

Every life is a gift from God to be lived to the fullest. It is a fragile gift that can be taken away at any time. I remember officiating at a funeral where the grieving widow told me, "He had just retired three months ago having worked two jobs all of his life. We had saved and saved and planned to start living after his retirement. We had plans to travel and really enjoy our lives, and now he's gone." There are no guarantees in life . . . neither its length nor its quality. If we have a tomorrow, it may not be better than today. Just ask someone whose house has just been completely destroyed by a tornado.

I will live today as if it is my last. This is not about gloom. It is about possibility. It is about the possibility of a fuller and richer life. It is about being mindful that on this side of heaven we are all terminal and that we all have a limited number of days. Neither the widow who lamented to me nor her deceased husband seemed to be mindful of this. They also closed their minds to the fragile nature of life. Together they felt that they would live many more days to spend all of the money they had frugally saved. They felt that they would have tomorrow to live as they had planned. Unfortunately, life does not come with a guarantee. Tomorrow is never guaranteed to anyone. Tomorrow is always a gift.

What we can count on every day that we live is that God will be with us. Look at your right hand...this is how close God is to you. Our lives can be lived in the joyful presence of God and not be so shaken by all of the negatives that come our way. A life lived in God's presence can be one filled with happiness and joy. God has gifted us with companionship when we invite it. Each day is God's gift to each of us to be lived fully for our pleasure and also to God's glory and in service to others. And then comes the day of days when Christ will return and eternity will be ushered in for those who believe.

Recently I saw an ad for a new computer game. It said, "This game will eat up days of your life." I thought this was a game that I would never buy. Computer games and entertainment are wonderful in moderation, but there is so much more to life. Life is more than just being entertained. It is about pleasing God. It is about working to have a meaningful relationship with all of my family members. It is about feeding the hungry and helping the poor and hurting. It is about working for issues of justice. Each of us only have a finite number of days to do this, and we do not know how close we are to the end of them. What if we only had five days left?   Should we chance using them playing a game?

Have you ever witnessed a soapbox derby? These are small, hand made cars fashioned and raced by youth. The cars have no engine so they race down a steep hill towards a finish line. The closer to the finish line, the faster the soap box car goes. Someone likened our life to a soap box derby. It seems like the closer we approach the finish line the quicker our life goes. As a kid it took forever for Christmas to come. Now, one Christmas seems to click by after another. Those of us who are older especially need to make the most out of our every day. Even the President of the United States gets the same amount of time each day as all of us . . . not a minute more or a minute less. Like the President, we too need to make every moment count.

Making Every Moment Count

I often like to think of my day as a series of moments. Each of us has just so many years made up of so many days made up of so many moments. I cannot allow my life to just slip by. I need to cherish every minute, for once it is over it will never return. Some moments are good and some are bad. When we take pictures with our digital camera, we delete the bad ones and save the good ones. Likewise, in life delete the bad moments and save the good ones to be brought up from our memory bank to be enjoyed again and again. We need to practice the art of selective remembering.

Years ago I led a group to England and Ireland in the spring. For the first six days of the tour, it rained every day and was bone chilling cold. By day four, we were in Ireland knowing first hand why they called it the Emerald Isle. With all of the rain, it could be nothing else but a dozen shades of green. The weather was just plain lousy, so it was hard to keep up our spirits. Around four in the afternoon, I asked our guide if she could take us somewhere to get something hot in order to warm ourselves. She took us to an Irish pub. Many of us bought an Irish coffee. One was good and two was better. The following day was cold and rainy, and once again we retreated to another pub. The Irish coffee was even better this time. After another fine time of socializing in the warm atmosphere and hospitality of an Irish institution, I began to worry that some of my guests might actually be praying for rain on the sixth day. Those who took that tour remember the fun moments in the pub. The six days of poor weather became less of a negative memory. So as the old saying goes, "When life gives you lemons, drink an Irish coffee or maybe two."

But how about when our living gets really tough? Even people living in nursing homes who are approaching death's door need to seek out the positive moments in the waning days of their lives. There may be few, but they are still precious. It could be a kind word from an aide or the visit from a family member. It might be remembering a beautiful moment from an earlier time in life. Receiving Holy Communion from your pastor is always a precious moment. A good night's sleep would qualify. For me, a dish of ice cream would make the list of positive moments in my day. As long as we draw breath, life is still a gift from God to be enjoyed.

Living in the Now

And what should we do with that last day that is ours as each day may well be our last. First, we should try not to waste one moment of it. We will not feel badly about that which we regret from yesterday. Yesterday's opportunities that were not seized are lost. I cannot be younger than I was yesterday. What happened yesterday is forever gone and must be committed to a kind and very forgiving God. The negative of yesterday must be forgotten and only the wisdom learned along the way remembered. We cannot go back to make a new start, but we can start to make a new beginning. That beginning starts today.

"I will live today as if it is my last." Forgetting yesterday, I will not spend much time either thinking about tomorrow, for I may never see tomorrow. I will not allow the today I have to be lessened by problems that I may never face tomorrow. If tomorrow comes for me, let it come, and God and I will deal with it together then. As the old saying rightly goes, "Today is the tomorrow that I worried about yesterday." Jesus put it this way, "Today's trouble is enough for today." (Matthew 6:34)

Today is all I have to live. When I awaken, I will begin by thanking God for a new day to live. I will rehearse all my blessings in my mind and thank God for each one of them. Then I will ask God to direct my path throughout the day. I will seek to please God in all of my doings and interactions. I will try to discover how God wishes to use my hands to help the less fortunate. When I read the morning paper, I will thank God that it was not me in the fatal car crash or the refugee in a foreign land. I will invite God's help in guarding my tongue that it might be used to edify others and not hurt them. I will look for "God Moments" when I experience God in a powerful way in my life. I have been blessed with today with all of its possibilities for happy moments and meaningful living.

And what else might I do with my gift of today? I will praise my God and learn from God's Word. I will hug my children and grandchildren. They are with me today, and I do not know if I will again have this occasion tomorrow. I will tell people I love, "I love you." I will forgive people who have hurt me, bringing healing to both of us. I will try to avoid people who are wasting my time as they freely waste theirs. I will seek out positive people. I will try my best to avoid wasting my life in long lines and traffic. I will not play many video games or watch much T.V. I will take care of myself. And when given the opportunity to do something good for someone else, I will try my best to do it. Every year, every day, and every moment is a priceless gift from God given to me to be used to the fullest.

This is the day the Lord has made, and I have decided to be glad in it and to live it fully as it may well be my last. I will endeavor to make today the very best day of my life. I will join the M.T.C. Club. That is the Make Today Count Club. Every minute I will attempt to do something significant. And if today is not my last day, and if tomorrow should also be my gift, I will thank God for yet one more opportunity to live another day at the highest level.

SEVEN

LOVE - LOVE - LOVE

There are few things in our lives that would supplant the importance of love. It is really the essence of God for "God is love" as the Bible points out. We first love God. We then love others. And we even love ourselves. Yes, we include ourselves within our sphere of loving. All three are important but all in the right order . . . God, others, ourselves. If God loved others, why shouldn't we love others as well? If God can love us, shouldn't we love ourselves as well? Years ago one of the most popular songs in my congregation's Vacation Bible School went:

> "Love, Love, Love!
> That's what it's all about,
> 'Cause God loves us,
> We love each other;
> Mother, father, sister, brother,
> Everybody sing and shout,
> 'Cause that's what it's all about.
> It's about love, love, love!
> It's about love, love, love."

Both receiving and sharing warmth and human affection is something which we all desire and need. Loving and being loved is one of the staples of human existence. Although physical affection is one way of expressing love, physical affection alone is not all that love is. Expressing love is a multifaceted endeavor. To discover how to be really good at expressing love, we must look first to the greatest of all lovers. God is that lover. God's love for us is not regulated by our response. It is always reaching out to us even when we turn our backs on it. Thankfully, God is a persistent suitor. God doesn't love us because we are always so lovable. God does not need to love us for God's sake. God loves us for our sake. We are in need of God's love. And God has given it to us generously through Jesus Christ. The Bible tells us that while we were yet sinners, God loved us. God did not love us because we deserved it but because we needed it.

Deeply Loving the Lord Our God

When we fall in love with someone, we have a great desire to be with that person. All day we think about them and hope time passes quickly so that we can hold them in our arms once again. We do things we think will please them. We are so very thoughtful and considerate. And we demonstrate our love to them through our actions. We also say with our lips the words, "I love you." To love God and put God first in our lives, should we not do the same? We desire to come to church weekly and express our love for God through worship. We deepen our relationship with God by reading the Bible. We frequently talk to God through prayer. We make ourselves and our gifts available to God and become God's hands reaching out to those less fortunate than ourselves.

I ask myself the question of how I would want God to love me. I would want God to love me in a deep, committed, and passionate way. I wouldn't want it to be a passing fancy and flirtation. I wouldn't desire it to be a mere infatuation that comes and goes. I wouldn't want God to love me sporadically when God had nothing better to do. Rather, I would want it to be a sincere love, a committed love, a hang in there when the going gets tough kind of love. And likewise I feel that the Lord feels similarly about the way I show my love in return.

Christian love is so much more than the everyday run of the mill love expressed through popular love songs and Hallmark cards. Christian love, true love, enters into the realm of God as we are grafted into Christ through our Baptism. We constantly seek to love the Lord our God with all of our heart, mind, and being. We daily welcome the Spirit of God to dwell in us. We seek to snuggle with God and feel God's presence. We strive to enter into the realm of the Almighty and experience the Kingdom of God on earth as it is in heaven. As we receive Holy Communion, we enjoy a foretaste of the feast to come.

Loving Even the Unlovable

Christianity in its purest form is not a religion but a way of life. The love of God in Jesus Christ permeates us. It inhabits us. It radiates from us. It directs our actions and decisions. True love is a willingness to give ourselves to another not for our own sake but for their sake. Love in its purest form is other-directed. It is not inward-directed. When another person's burdens and needs become more important than our own, that is love born of God. The Lord gives us the ability to love selflessly. Wanting to become a better lover, we open our hearts and welcome in the fullness of God's love. Then we are able to call up the perfect love of God within us and reach out and express our love to other people around us.

On their fiftieth anniversary, a wife summons the courage to confront her husband on their special day. "Dear," she says lovingly, "for fifty years of marriage you have been there for me and the family. You have been a good provider, and I know that you love me. But other than our wedding night, I do not remember a single time in these past fifty years we've been married that you once again said to me the words, 'I love you.'" The husband thought a long while and finally spoke, "When I change my mind, I will tell you." Whether or not this is just a humorous story, it illustrates that loving someone also needs to be expressed by saying the words, "I love you." Words of love need to also accompany acts of love.

On a trip to Greece where we walked in the footsteps of St. Paul, we visited the site of ancient Corinth where Paul established a significant church. We stood in the ruins of the marketplace at the very spot where Paul preached the message of Jesus Christ. I spoke about love to the group I was leading. I pointed out that love was much more than a sentimental feeling. It was an indwelling of God, motivating us and helping us forgive even someone who has grievously offended us. I invited those present to think of someone who had hurt them deeply, someone who did not deserve their love, but someone who needed it. I encouraged them to resolve to forgive that person and be reconciled with them.

Our Greek guide, Rea, had been listening to me. Later she challenged me by saying, "How can you do this? If someone wrongs you and it is not your fault, it is not humanly possible to love such a person." Rea understood human nature and was right. Our human nature is not inclined to love someone who has grievously offended us. It is even harder when this person does not care and therefore does not even ask for our forgiveness. I told Rea that it is possible to love and forgive even this person, but we cannot do it by ourselves. We must first invite the powerful love of God to enter us. Then God, through us, can do what we could not do alone.

When someone chooses not to accept my forgiveness . . . when I reach out my hand in friendship and someone does not take it . . . when I love someone and they do not love me in return, it is not easy. But it is necessary. For I am doing this for them and in obedience to the Lord. I need to remember the times God has continued to offer love and forgiveness to me when I was not ready to fully accept it. I extend my hand not only for my sake and their sake, but also for Christ's sake. I do it in obedience to God's will. This alone makes it worthwhile. Then instead of feeling badly that my gesture was spurned, I try to feel sorry for that person and myself because of their unwillingness to become reconciled with me. Love regulated by another person's response is not love at all. There are those times when someone chooses, for whatever reason, to not like me. Rather than not liking them, I choose to feel sorry that they are not allowing themselves to see and enjoy the better side of my nature. I am not perfect, but parts of me are pretty good.

In Victor Hugo's famous novel, *Les Miserables*, Jean Valjean is a convict who has spent nineteen years in prison for having stolen a mere loaf of bread. When he is finally set free, he painfully discovers that he is ostracized by society. The inn will not rent him a room; the tavern will not sell him a meal. Weary and lonely, he feels that no one will ever care for him again. Desperate, he finds himself knocking on the door of the local bishop. To Valjean's surprise, the bishop invites him in and provides him both food and lodging. He cannot believe the offer is valid and tries to reject the offer by telling the bishop his name and that he was a felon. The bishop responds, "You need not tell me who you are. This is not my house; it is the house of Christ. This is the home of no man except him who needs a place of shelter. What need have I to know your name? Besides, before you told me I knew it." "You knew my name?" questions Valjean. "Yes," responds the bishop, "your name is my brother." Love sees and respects everyone as a child of God no matter what his or her current life situation.

Love does not necessarily mean a personal liking, a sentimental affection, but an active good will in behalf of our neighbor. In other words God says we are to love everyone even when we might not be able to like everyone. The chemistry is often not right between two people. We might not like someone, but we are called by God to love them and to care for them nevertheless. Love shows constant goodwill in behalf of the neighbor. Love of our neighbor has no boundaries or exceptions. The bishop, in Victor Hugo's classic novel, extended his hospitality and through it God's love to an ex con. Like the Biblical Good Samaritan, we stop at nothing to help the neighbor through concrete and costly acts of goodwill even when this person is our enemy. God calls us to love others as we love ourselves. Like God's love, our love is never exclusive; it is always inclusive.

The Beauty of Self Love

So we first love God. We then love others. Finally, we love ourselves as well. When we are emotionally and spiritually healthy, all of us have a rather high regard for ourselves. It is both natural and normal to enjoy the beauty of self-love. The Bible speaks out against selfish love which excludes God and others. This is love with wrong priorities. Self-love is fine whereas selfish love is not. When we love God completely, and God helps us to love our neighbor, we must then also love ourselves. God's love for us stared down from Calvary's cross and spoke, "Father forgive them." If God can love us so deeply, we can love ourselves as well. The death of God's Son, Jesus Christ, was not too great a price to pay for our salvation. We are surely worth a lot to God to be willing to make such a sacrifice in our behalf.

Have you ever really thought how wonderfully made you are? We are often impressed by ever advancing technology. We now have artificial intelligence and self-driving cars. We almost take it for granted that our cars talk to us and respond to our voice commands. GPS has made paper maps nearly obsolete. There are so many wow devices available today with more being invented all the time. Yet nothing is as spectacular as we are. Sometimes I look just at my hand and marvel at all the things it is capable of doing. It, like the rest of me, is beautifully and amazingly made. If I can love my newest iPhone, why can't I love myself even more? We are the masterpiece of God's creative genius.

When God indwells us and helps us to be able to forgive others, God encourages us to also forgive ourselves as well. As we unload our negative baggage, our burden lightens, and our life becomes happier. If God forgives me and I am now okay with God, why wouldn't I also be okay with myself? The beauty of loving God . . . the beauty of loving others . . . the beauty of loving ourselves . . . together these three comprise the beauty of Christian love. "It's about love, love, love. It's about love, love, love."

Commercial

My latest book, *Love-It's the Greatest,* looks at the many facets of love that St. Paul eloquently wrote about in 1 Corinthians Chapter 13. This chapter is perhaps the most popular and most loved chapter in the entire Bible. It is St. Paul's love poem. The entire book plunges into the depths of love's meaning as shared with us through the pen of St. Paul. It is great as a devotional read and like *Living a Happier Life,* it can also be used for group Bible study. It will be available from Amazon.com in fall of 2018.

EIGHT

PRAYER POWER

Prayer works. I have witnessed its power during my entire life and ministry. Three years ago the bishop's assistant called me and asked me to be the interim pastor of a local church. Most people felt it would close in the next few months. I sensed that I was being invited to provide church hospice care. I prayed for God's guidance and help to keep this church alive and to not let it fail as so many other churches have.

The church had a $40,000 deficit with only $20,000 left in the bank to cover it. The full story of what happened is told in my recent book, *From Surviving to Thriving – A Practical Guide to Revitalize Your Church* (available from Amazon.com). The first thing that I did upon arriving was to telephone every family in the church and invite them to pray daily for Faith. "Just as you pray for your children and grandchildren, pray daily for Faith as well that it will once again thrive," I encouraged every member. I also asked them to introduce themselves to me the following Sunday at church. "May I look forward to greeting you next Sunday?" I asked each one of them trying to get them to commit to attend worship.

Now we did a lot of other things, but fervent prayer was the foundation of the revitalization of this church. We began by saturating this church in prayer. This is what God accomplished. In the first month, God motivated an avowed atheist to donate $1000 to the church. This was God's attention getter. The attendance grew by 25%. The $40,000 deficit was erased. The church's interior was refurbished with new carpet, pew cushions, and lighting by the generosity of one family. A new baby grand piano was donated to the church. The weekly offerings increased to the point of being able to support a full time pastor. We grew a surplus of $110,000. There was a special Faith Forward Fund established which received an additional $40,000 in donations to be used to grow the church. And one family put the church in their will for well over a million dollars. This is just one example from my years of parish ministry of how powerfully prayer works. And all of this took place in just nine months.

"The church is full of hypocrites. I can worship God anywhere." This was my father's thinking. He did not attend church for most of my childhood. He was a good father, a moral man, a hard worker, a good husband, believed in God, a former Sunday School teacher, but after having served in World War II, church was no longer for him. This bothered me very much. I wanted my Dad to be in heaven with me. I prayed for him every night.

One Sunday morning the pastor of my church preached a powerful sermon on why church attendance was necessary. I listened intently. I went home and shared what was said with my Dad. Then I told him how much I loved him and wanted him to be in heaven with me. The

Holy Spirit used a 13- year- old's prayers and witness to touch a 40- year- old combat veteran's heart. He attended church the following week and for the rest of his life. I look forward to joining him in heaven. Prayer works in our individual lives as well.

Prayer is Dynamite

In a rural church in Minnesota, there was a pastor who loved fishing. He was very successful and always brought back many fish. One of his members, who was not nearly as fortunate, constantly asked the pastor to take him fishing with him so that he might discover why the pastor was so successful. After refusing him many times, the pastor finally relented. "I will take you with me under the condition that you do not comment or tell anyone how I fish." His parishioner agreed. The long awaited day arrived. The parishioner came loaded up with all of his fishing gear. The pastor came with only a small tackle box. The lake where they went fishing was secluded. The parishioner decide to just sit back and observe the master fisherman at work.

Rowing to the middle of the lake, the pastor opened his tackle box and took out a stick of dynamite, lit it, and threw it as far as he could. KABOOM and dozens of dead fish came floating to the surface. He then rowed over to his "catch," picked them out of the lake and put them into his boat. His friend was stunned and stammered, "Pastor, you are not allowed to fish with dynamite." The pastor smiled and responded, "Now, didn't we agree that you would not comment on how I fish?"

Dynamite comes from the ancient Greek word, *dynamis,* which means power. Prayer is dynamite . . . powerful. And when we pray believing, the Holy Spirit uses prayer to powerfully transform the lives of churches as well as family members. There is no effective evangelism without prayer. When God calls us to go fishing for those who do not believe strongly enough to worship weekly, prayer is the power that brings success to our efforts.

Recently, a pastor told me that he and the members of his congregation take prayer walks through their community. As they see someone on the street, they pray quietly for them. When they pass a home, they pray for the inhabitants. Later, they visit each home, and among other things, they ask the people if there is anything that they would like the church to pray about the following Sunday. If the people they visit are not actively attending another church in the community, they are also invited to this pastor's church.

"The family that prays together stays together." This old saying is as true today as when it was popularized years ago by Father Patrick Peyton. Today, nearly half of all marriages end in divorce. When the husband and wife attend church together, only one in approximately ten end in divorce. When they also pray together, one in approximately twenty-five end in divorce. Praying together and staying together is more than just a nice saying. It works because prayer is like dynamite . . . it is powerful.

Anyone who has ever had a dog will remember how focused their dog was whenever they were eating something. My dog, Daisy, always joined the family at dinner time and observed attentively as every last morsel found its way into our mouths. When she was fortunate, something tasty was thrown her way. During dinner hour, watching and hoping for something was the only thing in the entire world that was important to her.

Martin Luther had a similar experience with his dog and wrote about it. "Oh, if I could pray the way the dog watches the meat. All of his thoughts are concentrated on the piece of meat. Otherwise he has no thought, wish, or hope." Whereas food is the most important thing in a dog's life, prayer was even more important to Jesus than food itself.

Throughout Scripture People Prayed

At the beginning of his public ministry, Jesus went into the wilderness and prayed and fasted for forty days. Jesus' life was marked with prayer. Later in his ministry as crowds gathered around to hear him preach and to be healed, Jesus would escape to be alone and pray. Jesus prayed for those who were dead, and they came back to life again. He prayed over a few loaves and fishes in a little boy's picnic lunch, and miraculously, there was enough to feed five thousand people. His life was a life of prayer. Even from the cross, he prayed that his Father would forgive those who had crucified him.

Not only does the Bible record that the Son of God was fervent in prayer, but throughout scripture we read that other people of the Bible also prayed. Noah prayed, and God sent him a blueprint for the ark of deliverance. Moses prayed, and God used him to deliver the children of Israel from Egyptian slavery. Daniel prayed, and the hungry lions' mouths were closed tight. In the fiery furnace, Shadrach, Meshach, and Abednego prayed, and God protected them so completely that not even the smell of smoke was found on their garments. David prayed, and the nine foot Goliath was defeated by God and fell with a crash to the ground. The thief on the cross prayed to Jesus, and his salvation was assured. St. Paul prayed, and dozens of churches were born in Asia Minor and Europe.

Everywhere we turn, prayer is both encouraged and practiced in Holy Scripture. In the book of James, we read, "Are any among you suffering? They should pray." (James 5:13) Jesus tells us to pray and gives us The Lord's Prayer as an example of how we should pray. St. Paul says we are to, "Pray without ceasing." (1 Thessalonians 5:17) Actually there are 650 different prayers in the Bible. Prayer needs to be central in the life for anyone seeking to live a happier life.

When we pray, we are making a statement that we trust there is a God. Atheists may need to pray but do not believe there is a God to receive their prayers. Agnostics may have a need to pray as well but are not sure to whom to pray. Believers in the Lord Jesus Christ know that God turns a listening ear to their supplications and always is as close to them as their whispered prayers.

Prayer is not a matter of always getting what we want, but it is getting what we need when we need it. Not everything that a child asks of a parent is in the child's best interest. The child asks the parent fully believing that the parent has the power to deliver what is requested. We pray to God with the same belief that God has the power to answer our prayers. We trust that God loves us. We trust that God has our best interest at heart. We trust that God has a plan for our lives. We believe that God is wiser than we are. Even Jesus in the Garden of Gethsemane trusted the wisdom of God and ended his prayer, "Thy will be done." Should we have any less faith in God's wisdom and direction for our lives?

Four Components of Prayer

The four components of prayer are: adoration, confession, thanksgiving, and supplication. An easy way to always remember this is to remember the acrostic, ACTS.

Our prayer should start off with the adoration of God. We begin by honoring God and saying to God, "I love you." We acknowledge God as our creator and savior. We bow before God and kneel as we pray as a sign of our respect. We recognize that we are addressing the supreme being of the entire universe and humbly come into God's presence through prayer. It is especially appropriate to prostrate ourselves fully before God to show our inferiority.

On one of my trips to the Holy Land, as we stood in the grotto of the Holy Nativity in Bethlehem, a nun entered and prostrated herself completely in front of the exact place Christians believe that Jesus was born. There must have been fifty others from all around the world in this small cave. It did not matter at all to this Palestinian nun. What mattered was she was standing where God became man. Everyone who is born will die, but Jesus came with the purpose to die . . . for her and all humankind. We stood as tourists observing. She came to fall down and pray and worship her Lord.

As we begin our prayer, we fully recognize that we are the imperfect in the presence of the perfect . . . we the created in the presence of the creator. We should never become so accustomed to God that we lose the sense of awe as we stand in God's presence in prayer. We are to willingly submit ourselves to God and to welcome God's direction and use of our lives. Early in our prayer we ask God, "Lord, what can I do for you today?"

Following adoration, we humbly confess our sins before God. We contemplate where our lives are not in harmony with God's will. We name these sins and offenses before God asking for forgiveness. We ask God for the strength not to commit these same offenses and to lead our lives in a way that is God pleasing. We remind ourselves that there is never a wrong time to do the right thing and ask God for the courage to do it. We also search within to find what we are not doing with our lives that God desires. For example, God commands that we feed the hungry and help provide for the poor. If we are not sharing from our wealth to help take care of the less fortunate, this too is a sin which we must both confess and try to amend. Prayer is something we do both privately as well as corporately during a worship service. Most Christians also believe that receiving Holy Communion is another important way God imparts grace and forgiveness to them. In most worship services, Holy Communion logically follows the prayer of confession.

Thanksgiving follows next. We remember in detail all of our blessings from God and say thank you for each one of them. The Bible is filled with commands to give thanks to God. Thanksgiving and praise go together. Our worship itself is an act of thanksgiving. We come to church first and foremost for God's sake. It is a time to praise and thank God for the blessings that we have received all week long. We thank God for the gift of forgiveness through our Lord Jesus

Christ. We thank God for the love we received from others in our lives. I am still on the green side of the grass and thank God every day for life itself. One should thank God for the daily gift of life at every age. Then there are the many special gifts that God has provided me. Naming them before God is important both to show proper thanks to God and to remind myself just how much I have been blessed.

While in seminary, I attended an evening worship service right before Thanksgiving break. The worship leader invited the congregation to take time to quietly thank God for their blessings. I began doing this and thanked God for members of my family and a few other things then said "Amen" expecting we would very soon move on to the next part of the service. Nothing happened. I started again to thank God for opportunities I had been given and for our nation and the privilege of being an American citizen and a few more things. Another "Amen" from me but the silence continued. Only on my third time of giving thanks did I begin to reach down into myself and truly offer thanks to my generous and loving God. God has blessed us all richly. It takes some time and much introspection to really pray a heartfelt prayer of thanksgiving.

The final part of prayer is supplication. This is the time we make our special requests to God. We take stock of our lives and ask God to bring healing where it is needed.

We often pray to God for what we desire. God answers our prayers by sending us what we need. We also pray prayers of petition for others whose lives need God's special intervention. We pray for the church both locally and throughout the world. We pray for fellow Christians who are being persecuted. We pray for our leaders both local and national. We pray for justice in our society where injustice prevails. We pray that good decisions will be made for the benefit of the earth we all inhabit. These and many other things we bring before our Lord in prayer. Then at the end of our prayer, it is well to say, "Your will, dear Lord, be done." In this way we surrender our will to God's and demonstrate our full trust that God will answer our prayer in a way that is best for us.

If we as Christians spend as much time praying as we sometimes do complaining, we would find less to complain about. During his life, there were times Martin Luther was so busy that he said that unless he spent several hours in prayer he had no hope of getting everything done. When our life is grounded in prayer and we embrace the power of prayer every day, a happier life becomes ours.

NINE

THE BLESSING OF FORGIVENESS

On October 2, 2006, Charlie Roberts, a local milkman, burst into a one room Amish school house and murdered five little girls and severely wounded five others before killing himself. He left a wife and children behind. In spite of their intense grief, the Amish community did something almost unimaginable. They attended the funeral of the monster killer of their children. They brought food to the house of his family and sought to comfort them in their grief. From their broken hearts, the Amish found the ability to love and forgive.

On June 17, 2015, Dylann Storm Roof, a white supremacist, attended a prayer service at a black church in Charleston, South Carolina. While there, he killed nine people. As they grieved the loss of their loved ones, some family members of the deceased said that they forgave Roof his heinous crime.

Forgiveness is most often not easy. Our eternal forgiveness cost Jesus Christ his life on a cross. Death on the cross was so horrific that the Romans had a law forbidding a Roman citizen from being crucified. Even as Christ was dying, he was forgiving those who executed him as well as all of us whose sinfulness made his death necessary. So right away we can point to how much we have been blessed by forgiveness. Our loving God provided a way that our sins could be forgiven through our faith in Jesus Christ. God's forgiveness was pure grace, for it was something that none of us either earned or deserved.

In a similar manner, the forgiveness that the Amish showed as well as the forgiveness families of the victims of the Charleston massacre demonstrated was Christ-like. In many ways, it was not human. It only became possible because these people had Christ dwelling in their hearts empowering them to extend their forgiveness. Knowing that they were forgiven, they became forgiving. It is an example worthy of emulating.

Martin Luther said that when God commanded us to love and forgive a neighbor, no one was excluded . . . neither friend nor enemy, good nor evil. Luther further stressed that even if a person is evil and does evil against you, they do not lose the name of "neighbor." This kind of loving forgiveness was in full view by both the Amish as well as the black families. When we harbor hatred and bitterness towards someone, happiness will dock elsewhere.

The world has always treasured the words of the wisest minds. In every age there are but a few words that have the distinction of becoming classics. It would have been tragic if the last words of our Lord had not been preserved for posterity to cherish. The classical last words of the Lord from the cross are so much more than sentimental phrases to warm the heart and to stir the emotions once a year on Good Friday. They are the product of a great mind and the expression of a kind heart. They also reveal the wonderful heart and mind of God, for it is the Son of God who utters them. They are simple words . . . no frills . . . words from the heart rather than the mind . . . words the church down through the ages has treasured among her most precious jewels. The first of these seven last words is the one we all need to hear the most. "Father, forgive them; for they do not know what they are doing." (Luke 23:34)

With the sound of hammer on nail fresh in his ears, with the cries of "Crucify him, crucify him," (Luke 23:21) still crushing his spirit, and while in excruciating pain, Jesus' first words from the cross are words of forgiveness. Others crucified before him cursed their captors and spit out insults on those who watched the spectacle of their execution. Jesus prayed to the Heavenly Father to forgive those of his time and all of us yet to come.

And before Jesus uttered his last breath, he said, "It is finished."   (John 19:30) Years ago, archeologists discovered a first century bill of sale with the same word Jesus spoke written across it. The Greek word was *tetelestai.* This word can also be translated, "The debt is paid in full." At the beginning of Christ's three hours of agony, he begs the Father to forgive us. As he breathes his last breath, he proclaims our salvation is complete, and the debt for our sinfulness has been paid in full by him . . . it is finished . . . completed . . . it is no more.

Without forgiveness we are sunk. Only the perfect can enter heaven at the end of time when Christ comes again. The Bible tells us that all have sinned and have fallen short of the glory of God. We need to be righteous and without sin in order to get into heaven. Unfortunately, many feel that living a good life will earn them a spot in heaven.

Let's suppose we were so righteous that we only sinned once a day . . . we got angry at someone, we had a bad thought, we failed to help someone in need. That would become 365 sins in a year. If we lived to be 75 years old, that would total 27,375 sins. The entrance requirement for heaven is that we have no sins . . . not even one.

None of us is perfect, and if we cannot recognize our own imperfections, others are quick to point them out to us. The story is told of a family gathered at the dinner table. The eldest boy announces that he is going to marry the girl across the street.

"But her family didn't leave her a penny," objected the father.

"And she hasn't saved a cent," added the mother.

"She doesn't know a thing about football," added Junior.

"I've never seen a girl with such funny hair," chimed in sister.

"All she does is read trashy, romance novels," continued Uncle.

"And those tight fitting clothes . . . in such poor taste," added Auntie.

"But she isn't sparing the powder and the paint," chided Grandma.

"True," agreed the devastated boy, "but she has one supreme advantage over all of us."

"What's that?" they all asked.

The boy smiled and said, "She has no family."

Sometimes our family can seem troubling as in this humorous little story. But often they are the ones to help us see the error of our choices and our ways. They are one of the primary places where forgiveness is both practiced and encouraged. In the case of our story, there is a place for forgiveness on several levels.

The Biblical Faces of Forgiveness

The word *forgiveness* comes with several meanings in the Old Testament. Each form or meaning further defines the term for our understanding. In Hebrew the metaphors of "covering," "wiping away," and "removing," are used to express forgiveness. Forgiveness is an expression of the relationship between our God and us. Sin destroys the relationship, and forgiveness is God removing or wiping away or covering our sins. When sins are forgiven, reconciliation occurs, and we once again enjoy the blessings of fellowship with God. Forgiveness is the removal of the barriers between God and us. We are called to repent, and when we do, sin is cast away by God. Even when we backslide and at times are unfaithful, God continues to wait for our return.

In the New Testament, the words, "sending away" are most often used. Repentance is also more prominent with the coming of John the Baptist and Jesus. We are to repent of our sins and believe in the gospel. And when we repent, we are to turn away from our sins. Jesus also says that as we are forgiven we are to forgive in return. In the Lord's Prayer our being forgiven and having our sins sent away only happens when we are willing to forgive those who sin against us. In Jesus' parable of the unmerciful servant, he stresses that we who have been forgiven much, must also forgive others generously as well. (Matthew 18:23-35) So to summarize, forgiveness comes to us when we have faith and repent but also upon our forgiveness of others.

The Blessing of Forgetfulness

In the Bible we also learn that when God forgives us, God also forgets our offense. So when we confess a particular sin on Monday, and confess it again on Tuesday, God does not know what we are talking about. God has not only forgiven our sin but consigns our offense to everlasting forgetfulness. God calls upon us to do the same. When we profess, "I can forgive but I cannot forget," we have not fully forgiven our brother's offense. A college once turned down the application of George Washington Carver because he was a Negro. Years later when someone asked him what college that was, he replied, "I just don't remember."

A very important part of living a happier life is to work at healing our hurtful memories. No life is completely void of painful memories of the past. Slights we experienced, mean words directed our way, goals not reached, broken relationships, poor decisions made, the death of someone we loved and so much more. These memories continually pop up and destroy the joy of the present. Like worry, they rob us of a happier life. This is why the forgiving of ourselves as well as others becomes so important. Forgiveness is the medicine that heals these memories. Like God who both forgives and forgets, this is a skill we too must continually work to acquire. Something bad forgotten can no longer raise its ugliness in our consciousness. Even if we cannot completely forget it, we can remember it less often by committing it in prayer to God. And when we have forgiven ourselves, it lessens the pain and adds to our happiness.

In a church basement, a plaque hung on the wall that read, "Forget, Forgive, For God." Notice that the first thing is, "Forget." Only when we forget is forgiveness complete.

Forgetting was listed first for emphasis since it is often overlooked. Forgiving and forgetting, when we are offended, comes with a blessing. Jesus said that he came to earth in order that our life would be abundant and happy. Harboring bad memories of past hurts robs us of present happiness. We need to let these memories go and not dwell on them.

The Blessing of Generous Forgiveness

On a group trip I led to Norway, we were on the bus heading to catch our next flight from Oslo to Bergen. We were more than half way to the airport when I noticed the couple sitting across from me seemed to be distraught. Soon I learned that the husband had left his passport and wallet back in the hotel room on the dresser. There was not enough time for us to return to the hotel and still make the flight. I quickly called the hotel to see if they could retrieve his wallet and passport. After it was safely in their hands, I arranged for them to hail a cab to bring it to the airport. We arranged a meeting place at the airline counter, and I described myself so that the cab driver could locate me. Without identification, my client could not fly.

All the way to the airport the man's wife loudly berated him. "You always forget everything. Why did you not check to see that you had these important documents before we left? I need to watch you as I would a little child.

You have ruined my whole trip." She went on and on non-stop for nearly an hour. Although I felt sorry for both of them, I especially felt badly for him. Luckily the cab driver made it just in time; the documents were retrieved; and the man flew with the group. The crisis was narrowly averted.

Three days later, the same man comes up to me as our bus made its way from Bergen to its next destination. With a great, big smile on his face and joy in his voice, he tells me gleefully that his wife left her passport back in the hotel room. Fortunate for her, I was able to have a bus driver from the same bus company, who was heading in our direction a day later, retrieve it and return it to her. Although both of these problems caused extra work for me, I could not help myself but had to smile along with this gentleman.

Be generous in your forgiveness of others. I hope the woman who berated her husband over his mistake became a kinder and more forgiving person after she did the exact same thing. When we make a mistake, we all appreciate it when the blessing of generous forgiveness flows in our direction. God calls upon us to provide such generosity as well to others.

Forgiveness is something we both need from God and from one another. Those around us also need to be touched by our forgiveness. Someone who abused us may very well not deserve our forgiveness, but we need to give it. Someone who belittled us in the presence of others may not deserve our forgiving love, but we need to give it. Someone who has shunned our every effort of kindness does not deserve another effort, but we need to give it. "But it is so hard to love and forgive some people," we protest. But who said it would be easy? Being a follower of Christ is not always easy. But being Christ-like is to be forgiving. When we are unwilling to forgive someone but rather plan to get even, we are only letting that person continue to hurt us.

Throughout my ministry, I have married over 500 couples. During their wedding ceremony, I talk about love and forgiveness along with an active faith as the cornerstone for a successful marriage. I tell the couple that love and forgiveness is never an if/then matter, "If you do this for me, then I will do that for you. If you do not talk about my parents, I will not talk about yours. If you forgive me, I will forgive you." Love and forgiveness is not to be contractual but generous. Rather than if/then, it is even though. "Even though your parents are tough to love, I will love them. Even though you hurt me, I forgive you." I tell the couple that I like to spell the word *love* differently than most. I like to spell it this way: *f o r g i v e.* As God loved us with a generous and forgiving love, we are called to do the same with one another. And with this kind of generous forgiving love, we will all live a happier life.

TEN

LIVING A "MAKE A DIFFERENCE" LIFE

"Will it matter that I was?" This is a question that most people ask at one time or another in their lives. All of us want our lives to matter. And it can in many ways. There is only one President of the United States . . . one pope . . . one Miss America . . . one American League Baseball MVP . . . one smartest kid in the class . . . one CEO. But there is also only one you. Although you might not be a standout, you need to be the best you, you can be. God calls all of us to make a difference with our lives. None of us are exempt. We all need to strive to live a "make a difference" kind of life.

In a *Peanuts* comic strip, we find Sally waking up in the morning. She jumps out of bed, walks into Charlie Brown's room, wakes him up and says, "Duck big brother, here comes another day!" Everyone has experienced similar feelings at one time or another. I believe there is a strong relationship between wake-up time and bed departure time. Do we visualize our new day as something to be ducked or as a new adventure with God? Are the first words out of our mouth, "Good morning God," or "Good God, Morning"? God wills that each dawn brings a new beginning for us . . . one packed with possibilities. Our life is a gift not to be squandered. We must be willing to become a person who makes a positive difference.

Greatness, as the world judges greatness, escapes the grasp of nearly all of us. The world's definition of greatness should not be the one we should consider, but we need to check out what the Bible says on the matter. Although there is little hope for all of us to become great as the world describes greatness, yet the possibility exists for all of us to become great people of God.

Father Abraham was one such person. Thousands of years before the birth of Christ, God came to a man who lived in a place called Ur of the Chaldees. His name was Abram, later renamed Abraham. Why did God choose this particular man and place into his hands a destiny which was designed to change the course of events in heaven and on earth? There is no certain answer, and I bet Abram did not have a clue as well. This much we know, Abram was not perfect. On any number of occasions in his life's story, his warts stood out. So we see that perfection is not the measuring stick by which God chooses people to be great and make a difference in life.

God's Unlimited Reservoir of Power Is Available

Then what are the characteristics of great people of God? There are several. First, great people of God are those, despite their weaknesses and faults, who recognize that God has made available to them an unlimited reservoir of power! They know that successful God pleasing lives are only possible through following the Lord and appropriating

God's strength for their weaknesses. They are common people willing to dream uncommon dreams. Great people of God, looking to make a difference with their lives, realize that eyes fixed only on themselves find few pathways to greatness. Instead, from their knees, they redirect their gaze heavenward where the King of the Universe directs all creation.

A Sunday school teacher, relating the story of the Good Samaritan to her class, tried to tell the story as vividly as possible so her children could identify with the poor man attacked and left for dead. Finishing the parable, she asked the class, "If you saw a person lying on the roadside all wounded and bleeding and half dead, what would you do?" After a long while, a thoughtful little girl broke the hushed silence by saying, "I think I'd throw up." It's easy for us to relate to the little girl's answer. But like the Good Samaritan, God calls each of us to make a difference in the lives of others. True compassion is not just having sympathy for another's suffering; it must also reach out with God's power and attempt concrete actions to relieve their suffering.

Seek and Listen to God's Direction

Next, those of us seeking to become great in God's eyes must seek direction from God and be willing to listen and obey the direction God provides. God called Abram into an uncertain future. In the biblical story we read, "So Abram went, as the Lord told him." (Genesis 12:4) Following God's command didn't offer any guarantees. God called Abram to be the father of a great nation and to become a blessing to all humankind. God called him to be a pioneer, to leave his homeland and those whom he loved, in order to strike out in pursuit of a distant dream. I am certain that Abram could not even begin to understand the implications of God's call. Abram went as God told him, the Bible tells us. Amazing, absolutely amazing . . . and faithful as well!

Isn't it true that potential is never fully known except in obedient action? Abram took God at God's word. He believed the Creator would be faithful. And God was. Abram became a giant on earth; his life made a tremendous difference because he often had his head in heaven listening to the voice of God. That which he heard, he believed, and his child-like trust led him on paths of obedience. By trusting and believing, Abram became the beneficiary of all the good things that God wanted to give him. He was not only blessed by God, but he became the vehicle through which God blessed all humankind.

Likewise when we get on our knees in prayer – a good position from which to hear God – and then demonstrate we trust what we hear by acting upon it, we will receive a blessing for ourselves, and we will be prepared to become a blessing for others. We, like Abram, must be willing to take an adventuresome walk with God into the unknown.

Have a Positive Vision

Great people of God are people with a positive vision. General George McClellan, Lincoln's commander of the Army of the Potomac during the Civil War, was one of the leading intellectuals of his time. Dubbed, "The Napoleon of the West," he had a spectacular record at West Point and had been cited for bravery in the Mexican War. He was a superb trainer of armies; his men loved him, but he had one very big problem. Little Mac, as his men affectionately called him, nearly always went into battle thinking he would lose. And he did, because his vision was failure. He achieved failure most of the time. It takes absolutely no effort to be a negative person. This is merely our natural, sinful, self-emerging. "Where there is no vision the people perish." (Proverbs 28:19 KJV) We cannot make a difference with our lives and at the same time be a negative person lacking vision.

When God is providing us an opportunity, we must seize the moment, for it may be fleeting. The story is told of an old, old man living in 78 A.D. He is sitting in his little hut in the town of Bethlehem. A young man comes up to him and says, "Ismael, Ismael, I just heard that you were one of the shepherds on the hill those many years ago when Jesus was born. Tell me, what did the little baby look like? What were his mother and father like? Was it really crowded?" As the old man played with the furrows on his brow and then ran his fingers through his straggly white beard, his eyes became misty and wet. His lips began to tremble as he said to his young inquirer, "Yes, I was with those shepherds. But I was too busy taking care of the sheep. I never bothered to go and look, and sadly, I never saw him." Having an occasion to encounter God, we must be ready to give up the good we are currently doing to discover the vision of the better that God is presenting to us.

Believe in the Impossible

Great people of God are willing to walk in the realms of the impossible. Seeing the impossible God has already done, we are open to the impossible that God can still do. Ethel Waters, the legendary Gospel singer, once said, "God don't sponsor no flops." Unfortunately, we fritter away much of our lives and move in and out of "flop hood." We waste so much of our valuable time and life moving ant hills when God is calling us to join in moving mountains. With eyes on God and seeking the Lord's direction for our lives, we seek to have our will become in tune with God's will for our lives. Then we will not be afraid to take a big leap if one is called for remembering that one cannot conquer a big chasm with two small jumps. One of the greatest discoveries we can make in life is that with God nothing is impossible.

There is a cute story of doing the seemingly impossible by silent screen actress and darling of the Yiddish theater, Molly Picon. While on tour, Molly heard some performers complaining about accommodations. "I never complain about any such things," she said, "My grandmother raised eleven children in four rooms."

"How did she manage?" someone asked.

"Easy," Miss Picon replied, "She took in boarders."

In 1900 a small advertisement appeared in a London newspaper. It read, "MEN WANTED for hazardous journey. Small wages, bitter cold, long months of complete darkness, constant danger, safe return doubtful. Honor and recognition in case of success. Earnest Shackleton." He said that he received an overwhelming response. Men were eager to accompany him on this perilous journey to the Antarctic. They were hungry to have their lives make a difference.

God calls each of us in a different way to our own kind of greatness. It just might be a call into the realm of the impossible. We need to be people of faith, for no one ever stumbled into anything sitting down.

To summarize, we must lay claim to God's unlimited source of power for our lives. We must pray to God seeking direction for our lives and listen to the promptings of the Holy Spirit. We must then faithfully follow the direction God gives us for our lives. And we must be willing to enter with God into the realms of the impossible. Then we will have the privilege of experiencing God more fully.

God Needs Our Hands

God's work needs our hands. We must be always willing for God's actions to flow through us. During WWII a statue of Christ had its hands blown off. The citizens of the town decided not to restore it. Rather they put a plaque in front of it which read, "Christ has no hands but yours." Each of us is a gifted person. Each of us has been given special gifts from God that can enhance both our lives and the lives of those around us. These gifts may not be apparent to us. We do not recognize them all at once. Some show up later on in life, even as late as our senior years.

It is just human nature to see more clearly the gifts of others than those we have received. We listen to Barbara Streisand sing; we watch Meryl Streep act; we observe how well Bill and Melinda Gates do philanthropy; we read of Abraham, King David, and St. Paul, and we are much impressed. We can easily think, "Who are we compared to them?" Taking nothing away from the famous among us, let's remember once again that God made us, and God does not make junk. Few of us will have the task of changing the entire world, but all of us are called to make a difference in the world we inhabit.

All of us can especially make a difference in the lives of those closest to us. A hundred years from now it will not matter how large our bank account was, or the size of our house or the kind of car we drove. But the world may be a better place because we were good parents to our children and were good neighbors to all of the people we knew. In the end, it does not matter how many years we lived but how well we lived the years we had. Daily we must seek to make a positive difference in things both big and small. For that which might seem small and insignificant now could loom large in the future. Abraham Lincoln wisely said, "When God measures a man, he puts the tape measure around his heart rather than his head." In this spirit, we need to care more than others think is wise . . . risk more than others think is safe . . . dream more than others think is practical . . . expect more than others think is possible. As we do this, both happiness and meaning flood into our lives.

As a disciple of Christ, we need to pray daily, "Lord, keep using me until one day you have used me up." Our faith is not something that we just have, but it is something that propels us to do. Our life is always one in which we seek to discover our Divine potential. It is up to God to decide when we will die; it is up to us to discover how we will live. We want to be everything God wants us to be. We seek to live a "make a difference" life. We need to live our lives in a way that the preacher will not need to lie at our funeral. At death, few are honored for what they received in life, but many are honored for the positive things they did with their lives. Living a happier life entails living a life that seeks to make a difference.

ELEVEN

THE POWER OF IMPOSSIBILITY

In my previous parish, one of the Sunday school children wrote in an assignment, "Because you are a Christian, you have the power of God, so you have the power of impossibility." Children often have an innate ability to express themselves in interesting and profound ways. The "power of impossibility" is one such utterance. We all know that which is impossible is something that cannot be done. But with God that which could not be done was done. God becoming a man . . . impossible. A virgin giving birth . . . impossible. Walking on water . . . impossible. Feeding five thousand people with a few pieces of bread and fish . . . impossible. Dying and coming back to life in three days . . . impossible.

The Bible tells us that the same power that raised Jesus from the dead is available to us as well. We can have the power of God, the power of impossibility. Another parishioner, whose husband received a troubling diagnosis from his doctor, said something equally profound to me. She said of her husband that, "He has to learn that to be strong he must first be weak." In order for her husband and their family to meet the situation that they were facing, they had to first admit their weakness to meet and carry their burden all by themselves. Their strength needed to be drawn from their relationship with God. Want to be strong, then first understand that the Lord must be very much a part of the solution to handling any troubling situation we face.

St. Paul writes to the Romans, "In all these things we are more than conquerors through him who loved us." (Romans 8:37) God never abandons the faithful. We continue to trust; we continue to work; we continue to hope. We continue to believe we will emerge from our problems stronger and blessed, and together with God's help, we will conquer them. And the impossible . . . it becomes possible with the help of God. The Sunday school child could not have been more correct.

Grasshoppers . . . St. Paul . . . Houdini

At Jehovah's instruction, Moses sent out spies into the land of Canaan. They returned and reported that they had discovered a land of giants, fortified cities, and a land flowing with milk and honey. Undaunted by their seemingly impossible task of conquering such a formidable land, Caleb, one of the spies who fully trusted in the power of God, said, "Let us go up at once and occupy it, for we are well able to overcome it." (Numbers 13:30) To this the majority of the other spies replied, "We are not able to go up against these people, for they are stronger than we. . . . To ourselves we seemed like grasshoppers, and so we seemed to them." (Numbers 13:31-33) When faced with a large problem, if we see ourselves as grasshoppers to be crushed under foot, that is precisely what we will become in the eyes of an adversary. When we are not willing to trust God and appropriate God's power to do the impossible, we are like the spies in the Old Testament story who saw themselves as grasshoppers and did not find their strength in the Lord. Therefore, God punished them and everyone else twenty years and older, and the children of Israel were not allowed to enter the Promised Land for another forty years.

Why go through life seeing ourselves like weak grasshoppers when God wants us to become spiritual giants? Unlike the unfaithful spies, while in jail St. Paul writes to the Philippians that he looks forward to what lies ahead of him wishing to reach the end of the race and receive the prize of eternal life. In prison Paul was chained between two guards. About every three hours they changed these guards. It is true that if Paul was chained to them, the guards were also chained to him. Imagine the assignment of sitting next to this individual on fire for Christ. Every three hours St. Paul got to share Christ with two more men. They were a captive audience for a three hour sermon. Paul believed what he earlier wrote to the Romans that all things work together for good for those who love the Lord.

The great magician Houdini was probably a better locksmith than a magician. He bragged that he could get out of any jail in an hour. A little town in Great Britain took him up on his challenge. His conditions were that he would be allowed to enter the jail in his street clothes and work without anyone watching him. The jail door was shut, and Houdini began to work against the clock. Houdini hid a flexible rod in his belt that he would use to pick the lock. Fifteen minutes, thirty minutes, forty-five minutes went by as the great magician worked feverishly at his challenge. Perspiring after two hours, he gave up. Exhausted, Houdini leaned hard against the door, and to his utter amazement it popped open. They had never locked the door. They had played a trick on the great Houdini.

The door was only locked in Houdini's mind. That was the only place that it was locked. Some of us when facing a challenge find that the only place in which it is impossible is in our thinking. That is the only place that the impossible is locked out.

The Power of the "I Can" Life

"I can do all things through him who strengthens me." (Philippians 4:13) St. Paul both believed and practiced what he wrote. Life is short, just ask any older person. The years between fifty and seventy go by as quickly as the snap of your fingers. In a way, a lifetime may only be about four snaps. However many snaps you have left, why not live them attempting something exciting or maybe even impossible for the Lord. Looking at a problem either in your life or perhaps in your church, begin by having a mindset that you can conquer it. As you face any challenge in your everyday life, begin by saying "I can." With a positive mind set, you have increased the possibility of your overcoming the obstacle immensely. Thomas Edison once wrote, "Our greatest weakness lies in giving in. The most certain way to succeed is to try just one more time." Every time I put on the lights, I can be thankful that he tried that one last time before he had success.

Another great inventor Henry Ford said, "If you think you can, you can, and if you think you can't, you are right."Do not be one who says, "I can't." Negative thinking rarely has produced any positive result. The world is full of negative people who sit on the sidelines of life and tell you and everyone who will listen why something can't be done. Do not be one of them; there are already too many. And that is not where the fun and excitement in life is to be found. Know what you want to accomplish with your life. Believe it is possible, and step out and make it happen.

The difference between accomplishment and failure is often perseverance. In many ways, the secret of success is for us to get up every time we fall down. Living an "I can" life unlocks the power in ourselves to accomplish a task. When the task is God inspired and blessed, we also unleash the power of God and even the impossible can be conquered.

God is bigger than any obstacle in our path. For the really big challenges in life, we must take our eyes off of ourselves and our abilities and firmly fix them on God. With God on our side, no one or anything can defeat us. When St. Paul was jailed, he was not sidelined or defeated. Even in jail God provided an audience for him to share the Gospel of Jesus Christ.

Punch Holes in the Darkness

Robert Lewis Stevenson, the great nineteenth century author of the classic, *Treasure Island,* was very sickly as a young boy. Every night as he lay in his bed, he watched the old lamplighters walk down his street lighting the street gas lamps. To him, as each lamp was lighted, it was as if there was another hole punched into the darkness.

This is a wonderful metaphor of our purpose as Christians. God calls each one of us to punch holes in the darkness of our world. When we are "I can" people, we punch a hole in the darkness. When we believe that even the impossible is possible with God's help, we punch a hole in the darkness. When we forgive those who hurt us, we punch a hole in the darkness. When we have learned that being kind is more important than being right, another hole is punched into the darkness. When we choose to be happy, we punch a hole in the darkness. When we see ourselves, not as grasshoppers, but as the powerful people of God, we punch a hole in the darkness. Worry less, another hole and less darkness. Pray more, less darkness. Love everyone, more holes and less darkness. Commit to making a difference with our life, yet another hole punched into the darkness of our world.

Martin Luther King, Jr. once spoke of the "fierce urgency of now." We only have one opportunity to live today. We need to choose to live it well and with a sense of urgency.

I once read of an author who was diagnosed with ALS, better known as Lou Gehrig's disease. His doctor told him that he had about a year to live. Normally he produced one novel a year. But now he had so little time left and so many ideas for new novels to write. In the next eight months, he wrote four new novels. As he continued with the doctor, it became apparent that the disease was not progressing as it normally should. Finally, it was determined that he was misdiagnosed. He did not have Lou Gehrig's disease after all. Although he said that he would not wish the misdiagnosis on anyone, he said that it changed his perspective on life. He now took his life less for granted and realized that it was a gift not to be used casually.

There is the urgency of now, so every day we need to look for opportunities to punch a few holes into the darkness. Such a decision on our part will not only lead to a happier life but also to a much fuller one.

Frank Ruddy

Google Frank Ruddy, and you will discover that he was once the U.S. Ambassador of Equatorial Guinea. He was also a classmate of a friend of mine at Holy Cross University. My friend shared this story about colorful Ambassador Ruddy. While there, Ruddy concluded one of his term papers with these words, "equal mind and equal content equal go." Meeting his college professor walking across campus, Ruddy inquired of him how he did on his paper. The professor responded that he got his usual grade. Then with a quizzical look on the professor's face, he inquired, "Mr. Ruddy, I'm not sure I understood what you meant at the end of your paper when you wrote, 'equal mind and equal force equal go,' could you explain it to me?" Ruddy answered, "Oh professor, it doesn't mean a thing, but you must admit that it sounded mighty good!"

The world tells us a lot of stuff that sounds good but holds little or no positive meaning for our lives. "Get the other guy before he gets you." "Cheating is all right, everyone does it." "It doesn't matter what you believe as long as you believe." "Who are you to think you can do that?" "That's impossible." Remember always that impossible is not a problem for our God. Our God is the God of the impossible. Impossible situations often produce acts of kindness showing the best of our natures. Such was the case on April 30, 2008.

The Portland, Oregon newspaper reported on a girls' softball playoff game. During the game, Sara Tucholsky of Western Oregon University hit her first ever home run over the center field fence. Rounding first base, she missed the bag and as she went back quickly to tag it, suddenly her knee gave out. Crawling back to first, she could do no more. According to the rules, she would be called out if her teammates helped her. A pinch runner could be called in, but the homer would only count as a single.

Now enter the impossible. Two members of the opposing softball team picked up Sara Tucholsky and carried her around the bases carefully helping her to gingerly touch each base so that the three run, home run counted. This unselfish act contributed to their own elimination from the tournament. The umpire said that there was no rule against this supreme act of kindness. When the two opposing players of Central Washington University who carried Sara around the bases reached home plate with her in their arms, the Western Oregon University soft ball team was in tears. "Win at any cost," the world tells us. The kinder and fairer angels of our better nature do otherwise.

The "We Can" Church

What if on the next Feast of Pentecost Sunday, instead of the regular worship service, the people who came to church were handed the names of inactive members, and as the organist played, "Onward Christian Soldiers," everyone marched out of church and went to visit them? This would be a most memorable Pentecost Sunday. Jesus did instruct us to go . . . to go out into the world and to share the story of God's love. Unfortunately, today many of our churches have given up. They believe that because it is tough being the church in today's increasing secular society that it is impossible to succeed. Because of this, some experts predict that as many as one third of all Christian churches will close in the next ten years. This does not have to happen. When enough of the church's members are "I Can" people, the church can become a "We Can" church. A salesman friend once told me, "The church has the best product of all, eternal life through our Lord Jesus Christ."

At Pentecost, the Holy Spirit birthed the church and gave it the power to do the impossible. On that day, 3000 people came to believe in Christ. The Holy Spirit's power continues down until today if we but seize it. Years ago in an Adult Bible class I was leading, I shared one of the stories from David Wilkerson's book, *The Cross and the Switchblade."* One man said that he found it hard to believe. "I've been around in Bedford-Stuyvesant and to think that two gang members would drop to their knees to receive Jesus Christ is unbelievable." I admitted that it seemed unreasonable to me as well. But to limit God to our reason is to put God into the small box of our minds. It is to suggest that God may not be any more powerful than we

are. But Jesus said that the Holy Spirit would give us power to testify about him with great effect. "These are not my words but Jesus' words," I told my parishioner. "We either accept them or we don't."   On the first Pentecost, 3000 people were baptized in one day. Gang leaders kneeling before their peers on a Brooklyn street demonstrated that the same powerful Holy Spirit was clearly still at work in the church today doing the impossible.

"Spirit of the Living God" is a beautiful song/prayer that has touched me over the years. The second stanza is like the first but substitutes the plural *us* for *me.* Here it is.

> "Spirit of the living God,
>   Fall afresh on me.
>
> Spirit of the living God
>   Fall afresh on me.
>
> Melt me. Mold me. Fill me. Use me.
>
> Spirit of the living God,
>   Fall afresh on me."

In conclusion, we now consider further the meaning of this beautiful song:

"Spirit of the living God" . . . God is not dead, not even sleeping. Our God is a living God desiring to enter our lives with life enhancing power.

"Fall afresh on me" . . . Yes, like the refreshing, life giving dew each new day, we welcome the Spirit of God's presence into our lives.

"Melt me" . . .   Melt away my sinful, rebellious nature that holds you at bay Lord.

"Mold me" . . . Mold me into the person you want me to be.

"Fill me" . . . Fill me with your strength and power to do even the impossible.

"Use me" . . . Use me until you used me up in the service of your church and your world.

"Spirit of the Living God fall afresh on me."

TWELVE

GROWING OLD GRACEFULLY

When my grandson got his first tooth, we all rejoiced, "Look, Tyler has his first tooth!" How many of us when we discovered our first gray hair rejoiced and told everyone saying, "Hey look, I got my first gray hair"? When a friend of mine recently commented on my getting predominantly gray, I told him that I dye my hair gray because I like the color. Do you know of anyone who has done such a silly thing and actually dyed their hair gray when it still had its natural color? Why not?

Why not is obvious. We do not like either getting or looking older especially after the age of about twenty or so. When asked their age, children proudly say, "I'm six going on seven." They even say this a few days after their sixth birthday. How many of us would proudly say, "I'm sixty-nine going on seventy"? In personal ads people instead write, "A young looking sixty," or "I'm seventy but look many years younger." Young in our culture is always perceived as being superior to old. But is it?

Now there is nothing wrong with being young, and likewise there is nothing wrong with growing old. Growing old is quite natural if we are lucky enough for it to happen to us. Old is not a four letter word. Really, growing old is a privilege that is denied to many. When someone younger than me might comment about my advancing age, I tell them that I made it into my 70s, but there is no guarantee that they will. When we were young, most of us thought that our growing old would take much longer. In reality, growing old is a good thing that happens to fortunate people. Long life is not guaranteed to anyone. It is a gift from God.

In Proverbs we read, "The glory of youths is their strength, but the beauty of the aged is their gray hair." (Proverbs 20:29) Also in Proverbs we read, "Gray hair is a crown of glory; it is gained in a righteous life." (Proverbs 16:31) Growing old and having gray hair is a good thing. As a clergy, I can especially attest to that. I have buried children, teenagers, young adults, as well as many men and women in their prime. Cancer has robbed me of over a dozen family members . . . most of them were younger than me. For me, it is a privilege to make it to the gray hair stage of life.

According to the Bible, growing old is a gift with benefits. With the experience of growing old comes the possibility of wisdom. Having put our foot in our mouths in our younger years, we older people are more apt to believe in the wisdom of thinking twice before speaking once. Biblical Job tells us that wisdom is found among the old and understanding comes with long life.

With the wisdom of age also comes a greater appreciation of time. We realize there is a finite amount of time that we all have this side of eternity. We must hold fast to time, and we must watch every hour and minute. Unguarded, it slips away. We must hold every moment as sacred and use it to its fullest measure. It is God's gift to use to God's glory.

The Bible also tells us that old is a good thing. An older person is a rich person . . . rich in God's greatest blessings . . . life itself . . . lots of life . . . thousands and thousands of days of life. Growing old is like putting money in the bank. When we put a little in over a long period of time, we wind up wealthy. Old people have the wealth of long life. Birthdays are good for you. Statistics show that those who have the most birthdays live the longest. Before he died at 83, my father spoke of how fortunate he was to survive the U-boats that sunk so many troop ships on their way to fight in the Second World War. He felt blessed that he had lived the longest of his seven brothers and sisters. Long life is God sustaining us and watching over us for so many years. Old means to be sustained and blessed over time.

A friend of my family at eighty-one and still in good health drove to Alaska and back from his home in Maryland. He did not care that it took him twice as long as most. He was celebrating life. He enjoyed our beautiful country. Seeing God's gift of nature was a much more pleasurable way to live his life than falling asleep in a chair while watching mindless T.V. Years ago, as a young man, while visiting our western National Parks with my family, I encountered many older seniors working in the gift shops there. I asked them why they were spending their retirement working. They said that they encountered nice people while working and enjoyed all the park had to offer on their days off. One elderly man commented, "This beats sitting in my rocking chair on the front porch of my home waiting to die."

Having Senior Moments

Now I am not suggesting that growing old is all fun and games. It is not for sissies. For some of us who find growing old particularly troubling, our next birthday will be the fourth time we have lied about being 69. Lucille Ball once said, "The secret of staying young is to live honestly, eat slowly, and lie about your age." The body, like an old car, slowly wears out. It does not run as well as when it was brand new. No need for surprise or frustration when faced with the negatives of aging. It is only natural. And then there are those senior moments. All old people have them. Rather than get frustrated by them, realize that they are quite normal for people our age. If you have ever been embarrassed by one of your senior moments, after reading below of the senior moment of senior moments, you will forever be able to say, "My senior moment was never as bad as that one."

An elderly Florida lady having completed her shopping returned to her car. She was startled to find four, young males in the act of leaving with her automobile. She dropped her groceries, reached into her purse, brought out her handgun. Screaming at the four men, she said, "I have a gun and I know how to use it, get out of the car." The four men left the car and ran away. Relieved that they were far away by now, she proceeded to load her bags in the back seat of the car. She got into the driver's seat. Her hands were trembling so that she could not get her key into the ignition switch. She tried and tried without success. Exasperated, she slumped back into the seat. It was then she noticed in the passenger seat a football, a Frisbee, and two twelve packs . . . none of which was hers. A few minutes later she found her car parked a few spaces away.

She decided that she had to go to the local police station and report her senior moment. The sergeant to whom she reported her story could not stop laughing. He pointed to the other end of the counter where four men were reporting that their car had been hijacked by a mad, elderly white woman, less than five feet tall, glasses, curly white hair, and carrying a large handgun. This account was recorded in a police log in a police station in Sarasota, Florida. There were no charges filed.

A Great Final Act

In most plays, the final act is often the best one. Why shouldn't we have a great final act as well? Each and every one of us hope that we will be blessed to reach old age, so why should we complain when we arrive? As people grow older, they often do not so much regret what they did in life as what they did not do. They dwell on their regrets and stop dreaming. We do not stop planning for the future because we grow old, we grow old because we stop planning for the future. A year from now we need to ask ourselves, what do we wish we would have done? Let's not be disappointed with our answer. As long as someone is drawing breath, there is the possibility of a meaningful and fulling life. C.S Lewis writes, "You are never too old to set another goal or to dream another dream."

It is popular these days to talk about bucket lists. For most people, they list nice things like sky diving or visiting Bora Bora or learning to dance better. There is nothing wrong with this. Go for it. I would also like to suggest another kind of bucket list. How about making "A Great Final Act" bucket list as well? Consider things like going on a mission trip with your church, writing that book that has been taking shape in your mind for over 50 years, adding your church as a beneficiary to your will, mentoring a child, and each day looking for ways to make it a better day for someone else. We need to figuratively set about planting trees to bring shade to the next generation.

We should work to establish a meaningful legacy. I would rather not have people view me as a nice old man. An interesting, awesome, old codger is more to my liking. I would like them to be thinking, "What is that crazy old Buzzard going to do next?" Why shouldn't we set out to have the last years of our lives be the very best? Most of the people who find growing old terrible are those who haven't done much with their lives. The good news is that your time isn't up until it's up. Thank you Yogi. Older people are often forgetful. Let me recommend a good thing to forget - forget that you are old. I know that nothing makes us feel as old as having to scroll down on the computer looking for our year of birth. Instead, let this be a reminder of all the great years we have lived. Old age is sometimes a challenge, but it need not be a death sentence.

Like a young child who enthusiastically lives life, we need to daily welcome this child-like quality. Just because we get old doesn't mean that we must think and act old. Henry David Thoreau writes, "None are so old as those who have outlived enthusiasm." We must keep our inner child ageless and carry a childlike spirit into old age. Living a meaningful life does not have an expiration date. God calls us to celebrate and enjoy every decade of our lives, even the later ones. We must do our best to make the last act of our life's play be the very best one yet. Let's have them leave our funeral talking about a life well lived to the very end.

Willing to be Surprised

Years ago as I sat in a doctor's office, a really old gentleman in obvious poor health walked in and announced to us all, "Surprised again, I woke up this morning." Every day we live is a surprising beautiful gift. When people greet me with, "It is good to see you," I respond, "It is good to be seen." Not one day or hour should be taken for granted. For when it is, we risk not living it to its fullest. However old we become, we must be open to God's surprises.

Remember Abraham of the Bible, he was ninety-nine years old when God visited him and changed his name from Abram to Abraham. At the same time God chose this old guy to become the father of a multitude of nations. Abraham already had his retirement party. The gold watch was on his wrist. The social security checks were being regularly cashed, and God visits and announces to him this huge responsibility. God tells Abraham the startling news that his wife Sarah, aged 90, who had been unable to conceive during her child bearing years, would now conceive and bear a son. From her son Isaac's ancestry, a great nation would arise. Both Abraham and Sarah laughed in disbelief. Wouldn't we also? God comes to this really old guy, and at the age of one hundred makes him the father of God's Chosen People. God asks, "Is anything too wonderful for the Lord?" All of us should shout with one voice, "No there is not."

There is divine possibility for every life at every age. Abraham and Sarah show us that people of faith are capable of wonderful and even miraculous things despite their age. People of faith do not retire from offering their lives in the Lord's service. At our Baptism, we began this journey.

Christian burial is the only retirement for those who love the Lord.

Growing Old Gracefully

By now I hope it is clear why I titled this chapter, "Growing Old Gracefully." This is a familiar phrase which probably means a lot of things to a lot of people. But to me it means holding my head high as an older person. I have been blessed by God with long life. It means being willing to continue in God's service. I see my gray hair as a crown of splendor. This is how the Bible refers to it, so this is how I see it. It also means that after I have lived my last day on earth, I will live my next one in heaven. By the grace of God, my sins have been erased through the sacrificial death of my Lord Jesus Christ. I grow old feeling loved by God because I have been richly blessed. I grow old awaiting God's next challenge. Abraham and Sarah could have refused God's great challenge, but they didn't. The most important time in their lives came at the very end. I will also look for the possibility that the most important days in my life may well be ahead of me.

When celebrating someone's birthday, I understand that some Jewish people have a custom of wishing them well by saying, "You should live to be 120." Whenever your next birthday is, let me wish you God's blessings and say, "You should live to be 120." And may you grow old gracefully realizing, with thanksgiving, how much you have been blessed by God. May you also live a happier life right down until your final breath.

Thirteen

LIFE'S FINAL ACT

This chapter is not going to try to convince you that death is a happy occasion for most people or their loved ones. But it will attempt to shed new light on death and dying and help you better accept death as life's final act. Living with a better understanding of death will also help you live a happier life.

Death separates and it hurts. When we love someone and lose them, we grieve because we first loved them. Our grief is an expression of our love and our loss. Grieving does not show a lack of faith but the depth of our love. The Bible tells us when Jesus heard that his friend Lazarus died that Jesus wept as well.

For me, life is like a hallway. We all enter the hallway through the first door which we can refer to as birth. The door at the end of the hallway let's say is death. The length of the hallway varies for all of us. For some of us, it is very short . . . 5, 10, 20, 30 years. For others, it is somewhat longer . . . 40, 50, 60, 70 years. Others very long . . . 80, 90, and even 100 years. What matters most is not the length of the hallway but what happens while we are in the hallway. For while we are in the hallway of life, if we encounter Jesus and fall in love with him, we do not have to go through the second doorway of death alone. We go hand in hand with the Lord. And Jesus presents us to God as one of his own for whom he died and rose again.

After my first year in college, I was desperate for a summer job. All I could land was a job selling cemetery plots door to door. Talk about tough jobs. From this experience, I got an education about how many people viewed death. For the most part, they just do not want to think about it and especially do not wish to consider it happening to them. "Why I just bought this house," one woman protested at the idea of needing a cemetery plot as if buying a house somehow made a difference. With a 30-year mortgage, the bank would surely not look well upon her dying. Another lady said to me, "Everything was going so well today, and now you came to my door." I felt like the grim reaper himself. I was glad I was not wearing black.

Death is not subject to our scheduling. For young people it is merely a distant rumor. Even people who are looking forward to heaven are not looking forward to death as a way to get there. Woody Allen once said, "I am not afraid to die, I just don't want to be there when it happens." Now I am not suggesting a morbid fascination with death. But to put it so far out of our minds as to not think about it ever is not wise either. There is the story of the husband who one day says to his wife, "Honey, if one of us dies, I'll go to Paris." Death doesn't just happen to the other person; one day it will happen to us as well. This is why I suggested earlier that we must all live as if each day was our last. It is up to God to decide when we die; it is up to us to decide how we live.

A Life Well Lived

A life well lived makes death a less fearful adventure. As a clergy, some of the saddest times I've spent with people who were terminally ill were with those whose lives did not have a sense of completeness. It was with mothers of young children. It was with men right in the middle of their blossoming careers. It was also with older people who spoke to me of time wasted and opportunities not seized. It is said that no people are more conscious about the fleeting nature of time than older people. *Tempus fugit* is an old saying in Latin that is still current today. It means time is fleeting and suggests that we must seize the day i.e. *Carpe Diem.* A life fully lived must be lived every moment of every day . . . every week of every year . . . every year of every lifetime. Yesterday is forever gone to us. Tomorrow is not guaranteed. Both the young and the old have but today to live their lives well. Being conscious that one day our lives will be ending should propel us to live them more fully.

Even after we die, a life well lived continues to matter through those who have been touched by our love and a world made better because we have cast our shadow upon it. Even though our heart stops, the love we have bestowed on our family and friends continues to enhance their lives. We continue to live in them and in their fond memories. Both of my parents are gone. But I continue to be blessed by them. Their words continue to flood my consciousness and enhance my life. And what they taught me, I have in large measure passed on to my children, and they are in turn passing it on to their children. My father-in-law was a man who embodied the word *kindness*. My life continues to be instructed by his example. The life of my grandmother, who loved the Lord more than anyone I have ever known, continues to witness to me and strengthen my faith. Likewise, I need to live my life with the hope that it will continue to matter and be a blessing to others after I am gone. As my passing is mourned, I hope to provide ample reason for people to also celebrate my life as one well lived.

What the Bible Says About Death

"A good name is better than ointment, and the day of death, than the day of birth." (Ecclesiastes 7:1)

"Even though I walk through the valley of the shadow of death, I fear no evil for you are with me, your rod and your staff – they comfort me." (Psalm 23:3)

"Jesus said to her, 'I am the resurrection and the life. Those who believe in me, even though they die, will live, and everyone who lives and believes in me will never die.'" (John 11:25-26)

"But in fact Christ has been raised from the dead, the first fruits of those who have died. For since death came through a human being, for as all die in Adam, so all will be made alive in Christ." (1 Corinthians 15:20-22)

"Be faithful until death, and I will give you the crown of life." (Revelation 2:10)

These are but a few of the very many verses in which the Bible speaks about death. Those who are in the Lord have nothing to fear about death but can find it as something to joyfully anticipate.

When we die, the Bible also speaks about our being asleep. Who among us does not welcome a good night's sleep? From the time we fall asleep until we wake up again, hours seem like a brief moment. Whether Christ returns a year or a thousand years after I die, it will seem to me as if I will be ushered into heaven instantaneously. And even while I lie in the grave awaiting Christ's coming, I will be resting in the loving arms of God. For God is neither up nor down but is everywhere. Even at death we will all continue to be with our loving God.

Dying with Dignity

A friend of mine recently told me of a family member who died of terminal cancer at the age of forty-eight. His name was Edward. He was a fine man of great faith. His daughter, Elizabeth, was getting married. He would not live long enough to walk her down the aisle. Just before he died, he had his wife and daughter promise him that after his death everything they planned in celebration of her wedding would continue exactly as arranged. Then he told her, "After my death, I want you to throw a banquet for those who attend my funeral, and when you are at your banquet, I'm going to be at mine with God. I do not want any tears."

After he was buried, the family did as he requested and held a banquet in his honor. A hundred people attended. On the banquet table was sauerbraten, potatoes, red cabbage, fried chicken, roast pork, applesauce, spare ribs, salad, bread, red and white wine, beer, soda, coffee, and cake. It was a sumptuous feast, but the one Ed attended in heaven was infinitely more so. Edward was a man who died not only in Christ but also with dignity.

Another of my friends, Ray, died in bed with the remote control in his hands. Since he was the master of the remote in life, his family took comfort in this. Grace, an elderly lady in my former church who walked up the steps to the altar rail every Sunday to take Holy Communion died at 102 in her sleep, in her own bed, in her own home. It doesn't get much better than this. We will all face death; how well we do it is up to us. If we are fortunate, it can be a time to witness to those left behind. It can be a time to express our love for our family and friends. It can be a time to say thank you. At the hundreds of funerals I have conducted, those mourning often recount the final words of the deceased. These words remain with family members for their entire life. So let's make our final words special and die with dignity.

The Grand Pause

Death for us who believe is not a period but a comma. It is not the end but a mere pause from this life until the next. As peaceful as a sunset is at the close of a beautiful day, so is death at the close of a beautiful life. Death is our final act; we need to prepare ourselves for it and play it with class. Lately, I was pondering the question whether we were actually dead before we were born? Whether the word *dead* is a correct word to use, we certainly were not conscious of anything. After we were born, our life was but a brief gift from God in the larger scheme of time and eternity. Our death is merely a pause in our journey which we began with God and will continue with God forever. That which lies ahead after we die is far better than what we have left behind.

In the German language, when one says good bye, they say *Auf Wiedersehn.* It does not mean goodbye, forever goodbye, but rather "until we meet again." It is the custom of some funeral directors to usher the family up to the casket to say their final goodbyes. For us, people of faith, there is no such thing as a final goodbye. Rather, we say to our loved one, *Auf Wiedersehn,* until we meet again in the Father's house. Ours is not a funeral march to a grave but the beginning of a triumphal march leading to the throne of God.

An English pastor tells the story of a memorable night in his ministry when he was called to a home of one of his parishioners. In the family were eight children, and one was dying of an incurable illness. It was apparent that the end was near for little Mary. The entire family had gathered in her room to be near her. When Mary breathed her last, her father said in a quiet, broken voice, "Mary is with the Lord; let us sing a hymn of praise." And with tear stained cheeks, the entire family . . . mother, father, and all the children sang with one heart and one voice:

"Praise God, from whom all blessings flow;
Praise Him, all creatures here below;
Praise Him above, ye heavenly hosts;
Praise Father, Son, and Holy Ghost."

And why shouldn't they? And why shouldn't we when we lose a love one? Dying was not the end of everything for either Mary or our loved ones, but rather it was the first day of forever. This is something worthy of praise.

The Little Blind Girl

A little girl was blind from birth. Her mother did her best to describe to her in vivid detail everything she saw. In the spring, she spoke of the budding leaves and the greening grass. In the summer, she told her of the fullness of the vegetation. In the fall, she related to her daughter the changing colors of the leaves. In the winter, there was the frost on the window pane and the whiteness of the snow. The little girl had an operation on her eyes, and she could see. When her mother came into her room, she said, "Mother why didn't you tell me everything was so beautiful?" Her mother replied, "I tried my best Honey, but I guess my words were just not up to it."

In the following chapter, I will do my best to describe heaven. But even as I begin, I am sure that my words will just not be fully up to it, for heaven is more glorious than any earthly words can describe.

FOURTEEN

AWAITING WONDER

I think heaven will be spectacular. I am looking forward to it. I am not wishing to rush it, for there is always the uneasiness of the unknown. I am enjoying my life this side of heaven and can be patient. But I am also thrilled that because of God's love and providing, it is definitely part of my future. For now, I am content awaiting the wonder of heaven.

Rick Warren in his book, *The Purpose Driven Life,* tells the story of the retiring missionary years ago who had returned home to America on the same boat as the President of the United States. Cheering crowds, a red carpet, a brass band, and a swarm of media welcomed the President home. The missionary who had toiled for many years in a strange land slipped off the ship completely unnoticed. Feeling self-pity and some resentment, he complained to God. He then heard God's voice gently reminding him, "But my son, you're not home yet." Our ultimate happiness is not here on earth but in heaven. Whatever our earthly life has lacked, our heavenly life will more than make up for it. As the old hymn rightly proclaims, "I'm but a stranger here, heaven is my home."

It is hard to describe what no one has yet seen. Now I know that a few people have died and after a few minutes returned to life. They have shared various things they felt that they experienced in heaven. No one truly knows how reliable these accounts are. The nice thing is that they all seem to be very positive. To the degree they are reliable, they are also wonderfully pleasant. These stories make for bestselling books and interesting movies. Our interest in these accounts is proof of our wonder about what heaven is like. The good thing is that they do not lessen our desire for heaven but only enhance it.

Let's suppose I could talk with you while you were still in your mother's womb. Labor begins and within a few hours you will be born. If I could then talk with you, our conversation might well go something like this. "Guess what, within a matter of a few hours, you are going to be born. Isn't that great?" If you were able to talk back to me, you might say, "I do not know about this being born stuff. It's warm in here; my mother's heartbeat provides me constant company; I get three square meals a day; I'm not so sure I want to be born."

If three months later I walked into your nursery and we could talk again, the conversation might go something like this, "How do you like being born now?" You might respond, "It wasn't all that bad being in my mother's womb, but that does not compare even a little to how beautiful it is being alive out here." After we get to heaven, I think that we will have a similar reaction to our life with God. Thinking back on our former life, we might say, "Earth was great, but heaven is fantastic!"

Whenever I do a funeral and little children are present, I tell them that heaven is such a happy place. It is like their birthday party with all of the gifts. It is like Christmas with all of its warmth and joy. But unlike our earthly Christmas, there is no such thing as the day after in heaven. Birthdays are not only one day a year but every day. Heaven is a place of fun and beauty and happiness for kids and for us as well.

What We Know About Heaven

By his death and resurrection, Jesus has opened up the possibility of heaven for all who believe. At the end of earthly time, we will be raised from the dead, and with Christ, we will become citizens of heaven. Heaven is the location of the throne of God and his holy angels. For me, heaven is more of a condition of existence rather than a place somewhere in the cosmos. It is where we have a living and personal relationship with God. There we will spend an eternity with God and with each other.

There are certain things that will be locked out of heaven. Cancer and death will be locked out of heaven. There is no place in heaven for broken relationships and hate. Poverty and war and man's inhumanity to man will be eternally locked out of heaven. When Christ comes again, we will be raised incorruptible. Our resurrected bodies will be new bodies. Sickness and heartache will no longer be possible. We will know one another and live together in peace and harmony with God and with each other. We will love God with all of our heart, with all of our soul, and with all of our being. We will also love each other with the same intensity of love. Heaven is the ultimate home of those blessed who die in the Lord. It is the abode of the righteous dead. It is the place where the Kingdom of God, which Jesus so often spoke about, blossoms and flowers to its fullest measure. It is a place of great joy. C.S. Lewis wrote, "Joy is the serious business of heaven." I can take that kind of seriousness.

Heaven is also the subject of so many jokes which often include clergy and lawyers and golf and dozens of other subjects. These jokes, though funny, probably add to many untrue images of heaven. Scripture speaks of heaven in images of life, light, peace, wedding feast, the Father's House, heavenly Jerusalem, and paradise. The paradise that Adam and Eve lost through sin will once again be all of ours to enjoy. And I also believe heaven will be a surprising place. For I believe that Scripture has not told us nearly enough about heaven to satisfy all of our earthly curiosity. Some of the things we imagined about heaven probably will not be entirely correct, and things we have never imagined will be surprisingly wonderful. Heaven will be the ultimate surprise party, and God will be the generous and loving host.

Many gravestones bear epitaphs. Some are funny like, "I told you I was sick!" Most, like my father's, hold eternal meaning. On his grave stone was written the word, *exchanged.* He loved the hymn, "The Old Rugged Cross." Particularly meaningful to him were the words:

> "So I'll cherish the old rugged Cross,
> Till my trophies at last I lay down,
> I will cling to the old rugged Cross,
> And **exchange** it someday for a crown."

He saw the gift of Christ's death as one which allowed his sinful life to be exchanged for a cleansed life with God in heaven. On another gravestone was written, "To Be Continued." Heaven is God's gift of something we all earnestly desire, that is for our lives to be continued beyond the grave.

A Taste of Heaven on Earth

Is it possible to have a taste of heaven while still inhabiting our earthly bodies? I believe so. The Biblical concept, *Kingdom of God,* is often seen as referring to heaven. In some cases we even read, K*ingdom of Heaven.* In the Lord's Prayer we pray, "Thy kingdom come, Thy will be done, on earth as it is in heaven." Here we are praying for the God of heaven to touch the earth with God's loving power and presence. Jesus' life ushered in God's kingdom. We who believe are part of God's kingdom both on earth and at the end of the age in heaven.

We also need to open our eyes and pray that we will see the hand of God so beautifully present in the world we currently inhabit. We need not ignore the world as we make our way through life but revel in its beauty. When we are open to seeing the magnificence of the world we inhabit, we also receive a foretaste of heaven as well.

Helen Keller, who became blind and deaf at age two, challenges us sighted and hearing people to be more aware of the wonderful world in which we live. She writes:

> I have often thought it would be a blessing if each human being were stricken blind and deaf for a few days at some time during his early adult life. Darkness would make him more appreciative of sight; silence would teach him the joys of sound. Now and then I have tested my seeing friends to discover what they see. Recently, I was visited by a very good friend who had just returned from a long walk in the woods, and I asked her what she had observed. 'Nothing in particular,' she replied. I might have fallen down had I not been accustomed to such responses, for long ago I became convinced that the seeing see very little. I, who cannot see, find hundreds of things that interest me through mere touch.

Helen continues to describe what she observes merely through touch like the delicate symmetry of a leaf, the smooth skin of the silver birch, and the shaggy bark of the pine tree. In the spring, she relished finding the new bud on a tree. For her, it was God's creation coming alive again.

The cool waters of a brook rushing through her fingers delighted her. If she can derive such pleasure by mere touch, how much more shouldn't we enjoy all of our five senses which are still alive for us?

I enjoy photography and looking at photography books. As I view some of the greatest pictures of some of the greatest photographers, I sometimes feel that I could have taken that picture. Some of the pictures are even of commonplace things. Perhaps I could have snapped the famous picture, but the problem was that I had not first seen it. You have to see it before you can take a picture of it. Renowned pictures are present every day of our lives, but we must open our eyes to see and appreciate them.

The whole earth is full of the glory of the Lord, the Bible says. Creation sings anthems of praise to the magnificent splendor and genius of God. God has created each of us and has blessed us with sight, hearing, taste, touch and smell. All of these are magnificent gifts given for us to enjoy. We pray that God would cure our partial blindness and that God would cure the disease of our deafness to many of the beautiful sounds of nature. May our senses of taste, smell, and touch reach new heights of awareness. And like the psalmist of old, may we know firsthand the heavens that declare the glory of God and the earth that proclaims God's handiwork. In doing so, we will have a taste of heaven even before we enter the proverbial pearly gates.

In Conclusion . . . Be a Happier You!

Your life itself was God's first miraculous gift to you. Have you ever wondered how come you are? Do you consider your being alive as a matter of luck or a matter of miraculous, divine design? The Bible suggests the latter. But let us first consider it. What are the chances that your parents would first meet, then fall in love, get married, then at a particular moment in time conceive you, and you would be born? Each of you is an individual, one of a kind person of the over seven billion people who inhabit the earth. Of all these people, there is no one identical to you. That makes you pretty special. You are here reading this book right now, so you are alive and therefore blessed. The miracle of your life is to be enjoyed and cherished both this side of heaven and finally into eternity.

Living a happier life is something we should all strive to do. There are many ways to achieve this. Hopefully those touched upon in this book will help you get there. So tonight, go to bed having wrung from today everything it has to offer and commit yourself to God's providence while you are sleeping. In the morning, wake up with a smile on your face full of joyful anticipation of the new day gifted you by God. Then with great determination, make it a great day on your journey to living a happier life.

About the Author

John Krahn has been a pastor for nearly fifty years. He pastored the largest multi-staffed Lutheran church in New York for eighteen years. Currently he is working as a church consultant specializing in stewardship and evangelism. He is a prolific writer. During his long ministry, he has been the CEO of a Lutheran social service agency, an Army Chaplain, the Director of Admissions at a Lutheran high school, an Interim Pastor at several churches, and owned his own business. He is a much published author and a sought-after speaker leading workshops nationally and internationally.

Krahn holds a Doctorate in Divinity Degree from New York Theological Seminary, New York; a Masters in Divinity Degree from Concordia Seminary, St. Louis; a Master's Degree in Theological Studies from Union Seminary, New York; a Master's Degree in Education from Columbia University, New York; and a Bachelor of Arts Degree from Concordia Senior College, Indiana.

Krahn is married with two children and three grandchildren. He believes that our God who is behind us is greater than the challenges which are before us.

Made in the USA
Middletown, DE
19 May 2022

65864886R00089